Hints & Tips
for Trainers, Instructors, Professors and Lecturers
with
added tips
for
Blended and e-Learning

Gerard A. Prendergast

Grosvenor House
Publishing Limited

This book is published by
Grosvenor House Publishing Ltd
Link House
140 The Broadway, Tolworth, Surrey, KT6 7HT.
www.grosvenorhousepublishing.co.uk

A CIP record for this book
is available from the British Library

ISBN 978-1-78623-273-1

Acknowledgements

I would like to thank my wife, Janet, Jonathan Backhouse and Mick Crabtree for their tremendous support, encouragement and help in producing this book

I also acknowledge the debt I owe to the many Instructors, Trainers and Adult Educators that I have worked with over the years. When training and coaching many of these fine people, I have picked up so many good practices, which I have included as hints and tips in this book.

Foreword

As Chairman of John M. Campbell & Co., premier training company in the Gas Processing Industry, I have had the privilege of meeting many instructors and many train the trainers from around the world. The "secret sauce" of providing effective adult learning opportunities has been a continual search for our company. I have known Gerard Prendergast since 2001 when we asked him to develop processes and procedures for improving the quality and performance of our instructors. Gerard brought innovative ways of helping our instructors to improve their skills. He added considerably to the way we recruited our professional Engineers and helped us share the "secret sauce recipe."

The advent of e-learning was championed by Gerard in our company and led to assisting our accomplished trainers with gaining new skills. This book attempts to gather both the theory of how to provide both in-person and online training with the best practical methods. I hope that you find that this book offers a clear path to implementation of effective adult knowledge transfer for those involved in managing, designing or providing adult learning opportunities.

Larry L. Lilly

President EC&I at CDI Engineering

Introduction

This book is designed to give new and experienced instructors and trainers hints and tips to make their training sessions more effective. There is also a section on how to implement and train Instructors and trainers in blended and online learning. It is a useful guide for training managers as well.

The hints and tips in this book, cover:

- How to get participant 'Buy in' to what you are teaching
- How adults learn
- Course Design and the importance of measurable Objectives
- Exercises to open your course effectively
- Exercises to find out what your participants want from your course
- How to run small group exercises
- How to debrief exercises effectively
- Dealing with questions effectively
- How to ask effective questions
- The use of and reading body language to enhance your effectiveness
- Listening skills
- Delivery techniques
- Aids to help you deliver your courses

- Coping with different learning styles
- Dealing with difficult participants and Classroom problems
- Dealing with different cultures when teaching
- Implementing blended or online courses
- How to be an effective blended or online trainer
- Dealing with participants in online and blended courses
- Course evaluation sheets
- Concluding your course effectively
- Evaluating your own performance
- Helping your course participants to use the knowledge learned post course

In this book, **I use the term Trainer to mean Instructor and Tutor too.** Whilst working in the South East of the United States, I was told that local people considered that instructors trained people and trainers trained animals. If that is truly so, I ask such people for their forgiveness.

If you are an experienced trainer, you may already use some of the hints and tips shown in this book, but I will be disappointed if you do not get at least 10 new ideas, tips or exercise from reading this book.

You will see that I advocate participative training methods throughout this book. This is because in my experience adults want to be involved. They insist on being treated with respect. They get bored with being talked at or to and want to take an active part in their training.

I hope that this book will become a useful resource for trainers generally. You may consider, that by re reading parts of it, every so often, you will remind yourself about things you are not using in your training courses. You do not have to start at the beginning, but dip into any section that you think you may benefit from, at a particular time.

At the start of each chapter, you will see a list of things I hope you achieve from reading that chapter. At the end of each chapter, I will ask you to list the three most important ideas you take from the chapter. By doing this, it will help you to remember the most important points of what you have just read.

I hope this book:
Makes you think about your training
Gives you tips you want to use
Increases your ability as a trainer.

Gerard Prendergast June 2018

GERARD A. PRENDERGAST B B.Sc. (Hons), F.Inst. L.M., DipSysPrac (Open)

Gerard Prendergast is the founding member of and was the Managing Director for ABACUS LEARNING SYSTEMS Ltd

Mr. Prendergast has been concentrating on developing the open and flexible learning aspects of education and training, especially the delivery of training using Computer Mediated Communication and Blended Cooperative Learning. He has trained Educators from many Universities, Colleges of both Higher and Further Education, and trainers from industry and commerce, in the UK and abroad. As a learning advisor to the PetroSkills, he has helped to devised their Instructor development procedure. This includes instructor training and instructional quality control. Mr. Prendergast is an Open University Technology Honors Graduate and he has completed the post Graduate Online Education and Training' Course run by the Institute of Education, London University. He has been a visiting tutor on that course and has also been a visiting tutor for the British Open University's 'Teaching & Learning On-Line' course, for a number of years. He has been an Advisor to The Management Institute, University of Ulster on Online Learning, and has carried out consultancy for the British Inland Revenue service, in ways to deliver training by Computer Mediated Communication. He has held various workshops on e-learning throughout Germany and also at The Croatian Academic and Research Network and with the John M. Campbell & Company, Oklahoma, USA.

A fellow of the Institute of Leadership and Management for many years and has conducted Management training for Industrial clients.

Between2002 and 2015, he has been the Consultant Instructor Development specialist/ Learning Advisor for John. M Campbell & Company, Norman, Oklahoma, USA, A company specialising in International Gas Processing Training. He currently runs workshops on Training for various organisations worldwide.

Contents

Part I. Face-to-Face Training

Getting 'Buy in' at the Start
or
Getting Participants in the right frame of mind

In reading this chapter, we hope you achieve the following benefits:

You will be able to: -

1. Explain why active participant training helps learning
2. List some ways to encourage active involvement by course participants
3. List activities that encourage active participation
4. Demonstrate ways to establish what learning participants want from the course
5. List the advantages and disadvantages of various room layouts

Experienced trainers recognise that, by actively involving their course participants, they will achieve a much higher degree of learning. **Professional workers** expect to have some say in the learning in which they are involved. There has been some recognition that lecture based training was failing to keep many participants attention.

It was also recognised that that form of training failed to motivate some different types of learners.

People who feel relaxed and in a safe environment tend to participate more, remember more and learn more. So if we can create an atmosphere, where participants feel that they are valued, their opinions matter and they feel safe to express their views, they will gain much more from any training session. Active involvement by participants will result in effective learning, because they take responsibility for their own learning.

In order to engender a '**safe learning environment**' the trainer needs to actively promote this, from the very start. **By having a warm greeting process** to welcome participants to the classroom, you will start to encourage the right atmosphere. It is helpful to greet everyone individually, as they enter the training room, building a personal connection at this stage. It is important that you are seen as open and welcoming on introduction. The chapter on Body language has some valuable advice about this.

Distractions

Your participants will come to the course, hopefully leaving behind their personal day-to-day concerns, but this cannot be guaranteed, even if the individual participants wish to be able to do so. It helps to promote the 'Safe Learning Environment" if the trainer can minimise some of these concerns, then. The trainer should request that cell phones, computers, and digital tablets be switched of or at least set to 'Silent" (See "Setting the Course Ground Rules" later in this chapter)

You might request, if the need arises for a call to be to answered, that the participant leave the room so as to alleviate any distraction.

Many trainers start building a rapport even before the course starts. This is often achieved by sending a **welcome letter** or email to each individual. As well as setting out the course objectives, location, time and suggest dress code, it should emphasise the participative nature of the course. Mention the fact that you will run small group work and exercises. Such a communication will help to start setting the tone of the course. However, it has been my experience that far too often, letters sent to companies for their employees attending the course fail to reach the prospective participants and you should take this into account. In my view it is still worthwhile sending out letters and emails, where you have email addresses. I usually include an item in the letter about the dress code expected. I suggest that participants adopt a 'smart casual' dress and that ties are optional. I stress that I wish people to be relaxed.

How you are dressed can have an effect on the atmosphere on the course. Different cultures may have an effect on how your clothing is perceived. I have found that dressing in a 'smart casual' way, usually covers most cultural requirements. If you are a lady teaching in the Middle East, or have a number of participants from that region, then it may be wise to ensure your arms are covered. The more informal you can be, taking account of the cultural issues, the more that participants are likely to relax, which is good for the learning environment,

Participants will then start to make judgements about you and the course you are about to deliver, when they first meet you. Trainers must display a degree of confidence and optimism that the course will be enjoyable and achieve the required learning. Too often, trainers' rush into giving the outline of the course first, rather than working on making people feel relaxed, and giving them some say in what they want or need to learn.

Room Layout

How a training room venue is laid out will have an enormous impact on the 'Safe Learning Environment' and the amount of interaction that will/will not occur. Whilst it is recognised that the trainer does not always have the power to determine the layout of the training room, where possible the trainer should try and get the most suitable layout in order to help the participants meet their learning needs. Unfortunately, often what the client provides will determine what can be achieved and often compromises may have to be made. That said, the following considerations are important:

1. How many Participants on the course?
   This will determine the size of the room you will need.
2. What learning activities will they be undertaking? Small group activities will require tables for teams to work around or break out rooms and each team will need a flip chart. If team work is carried out the in training room, it is important that the participants can all see the main screen and hear the trainers

Tip: When setting up your room physically go to the extremes of the room and make sure you can read the screen clearly. It is also helpful to test the acoustics.

3. What are the physical attributes of the training room?

    This is important, as it may affect the participants ability to see hear and learn comfortably. Such things as: pillars, Windows (distraction opportunities and too much light which may affect the screen presentations). Narrow or wide rooms also can affective the participants' ability to learn comfortably. Large group activities may be hard to accommodate in some rooms

4. The shape of the room will often determine the trainer's position at the front of the room. Please try and avoid using a lectern as this often ends up being a communication barrier between the trainer and the participants. Having a table for the Digital projector and the Trainer's computer is desirable, as is a side table for hand-outs and other material. A chair for the trainer to use on rare occasions can also be useful.

5. Check how to control the temperature of the room before the class starts. It is better to start with a slightly colder room, as the temperature will increase as more people gather.

6. For use of posters and other training aids please see the chapter entitled '**Training aids and how to use them.**"

7. Check on potential distractions such as fire alarm tests or contractors working nearby

8. Do you need to consider where to place participants with visual or hearing impairment?

Figure 1: Classroom Setup

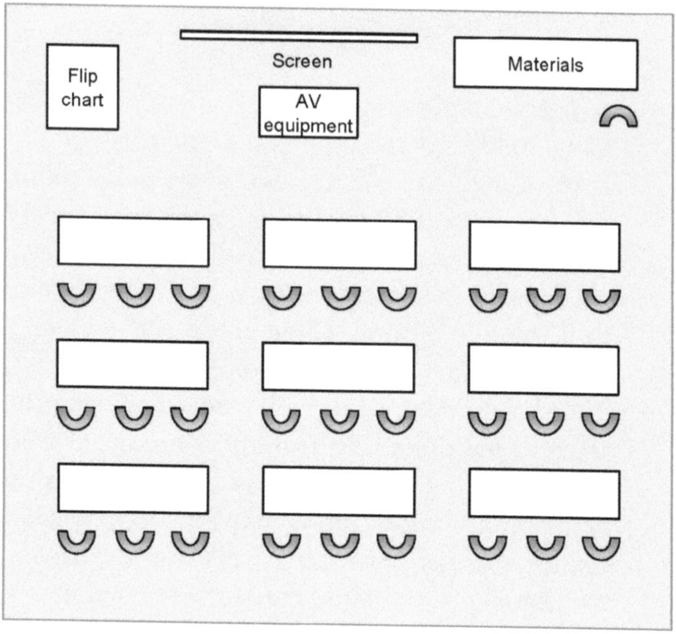

This set up is the traditional setup in many training venues.

Advantage:

Participants should be able to see the Trainer and the screen clearly.

Disadvantage

Difficult to get Participants into groups easily
Tends to inhibit information sharing

Figure 2: Classroom layout U shape

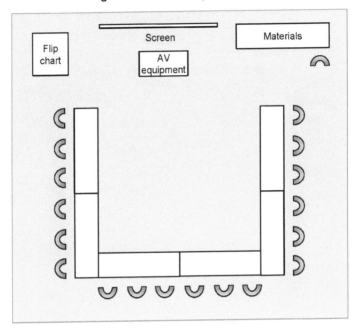

Advantages

1. The trainer can move close to all the participants by using the space in the middle of the U
2. By some of the participants moving their chairs into the middle of the U, they end up with three group-working tables. This will work for up to 18 participants

Disadvantages

1. Hard to use for group work with more than 18 participants without additional break out rooms or other tables in the Class room

2. Some Participants may find looking at the screen uncomfortable, as they have to look to their right or left, depending on where they are sitting

Figure 3: Classroom layout Chevron shape

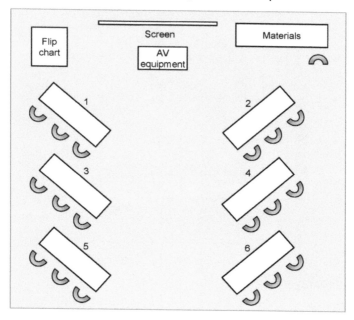

Advantages

1. This layout can accommodate more participants
2. Each table can be used for small group working without moving table
3. All Participants are able to see the screen and the trainer easily
4. Trainer can get close to the participants
5. By labelling tables with number or letter it avoids confusion as to where participants need to be to form new groups

Disadvantage

1. Not the best layout for initiating group discussion

Figure 4: Classroom layout Round Tables

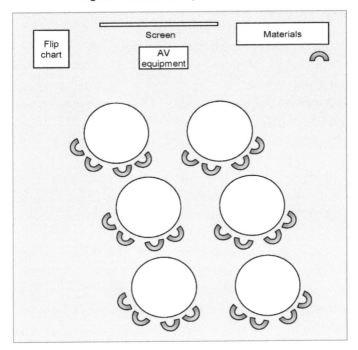

Advantages

1. This layout can accommodate more participants
2. Each table can be used for small group working without moving table
3. All Participants are able to see the screen and the trainer easily
4. Trainer can get close to the participants
5. Best shape for initiating group discussion

6. By labelling tables with number or letter it avoids confusion as to where participants need to be to form new groups

Disadvantage

Requires more space than most layouts

A similar set up to the round table one is where Rectangular Tables are used. This does require even more space, but has similar advantages to the round table setup.

If there is a large U shape setup you can add some rectangular tables in a chevron shape in the middle of the U. I found this to appear somewhat claustrophobic

Trainers need to be able to adapt the training room that they are given. Unfortunately this is the real world. How the room is laid out will have a real affect on how participants perform. The effect of the room layout is often very much underestimated by trainers. The importance of this is why I have included it in the opening chapter of this book.

Your Classroom Position

Where you stand or site in a classroom can affect the atmosphere. When presenting, you may need to stand. Where possible, try and face to participants. If you are using a PowerPoint or Keynote presentation, then place your computer between you and the participants.

That way you can see what will be on the screen mirrored on your computer and still see the reactions of your audience. When possible move away from you computer, when asking a question or introducing an activity. When trying to promote a discussion, it helps to sit down. Try not to anchor yourself in one position.

Refreshments

Having a variety of refreshments available will add a positive aspect to how the participants view the course and the trainer. Having desk sweets (some of which are sugar free), hot and cold drinks and during breaks some cakes and pastries help participants enjoy the learning experience.

Tidiness

If you want the best results from your participants you must keep their environment reasonably tidy. It is important to make sure that any discarded material is removed at the end of each day. You should be in the classroom at least 15 minutes before class starts and ensure that the classroom looks tidy, you have enough Flip Chart pads and marker pens and any hand-outs need for the day's sessions are to hand.

Security

Unfortunately, thefts from classrooms do occur, especially in city environments. You should warn participants to be on their guard and to take care of their possessions. It is advisable to state that **you and your company are not responsible if items go missing from the classroom.**

Tip: Arrange with the Hotel Staff or location Reception Desk staff for your training Room to be locked, if you leave it for lunch breaks and insist that they only agree to open it for you (or a designated Participant). Too often Staff have allowed someone posing as a course Participant into classrooms during lunch, who then proceed to steal valuable items

Personal Introductions

What are the benefits of self-introduction?
Think about this for a minute or so.

I believe personal introduction achieve the following:

1. Helps to bond the group.
2. Gets groups members to realise what they have in common.
3. Gets group member to realise what expertise others in the group may have
4. Helps you, the Trainer/ Instructor, see who is extrovert or introvert.
5. Helps you, the Trainer/ Instructor, start to understand what the attitude of the individual is.

Tip: I Use 'Tent Name Table Cards (Stiff card that can be folded in half so it can be displayed on each desk) I ask each Participant to use a large Marker pen to write on the card the name they like to be call, and then to place it on the desk so that I can see it.

Introduction Exercise

If the Trainer gives a few headings to be covered during the personal introductions then this often cuts down the time taken to run this exercise. I usually ask people to use the following headings which I display on the screen, using a PowerPoint slide, when they introduce themselves. An alternative is to put them in pairs to share this information when they introduce each other, this usually cuts down the time spent on each introduction as the person sticks to the facts and does not elaborate:

The headings I use are:

- **Name** and what they like to be called.
- **Their Job/ Role** and how long they have been in their current role. This is useful because you may be able to get them to share various experiences during the course. It also allows other participants to identify individuals with whom they may wish to share information.
- **Family circumstances.** This can be useful especially if participants have very young children or relatives with problems, as this may affect their course participation.
- **Hobbies / Interest.** This often leads to real surprises and again helps to create interest.

Tip: I find it helpful to draw **a seating plan,** prior to personal introduction session. When participants introduce themselves I annotate the seating plan with the following information: The name they like to be called, their job and work role and sometimes their hobbies and interests. This information helps future one-to-one conversations.

I start the debriefing part of this exercise by introducing myself. I tell them what I like to be called and a brief outline of where I come from. I give them a brief outline of my work experiences and education to emphasise why I am qualified to run this course. I also mention my hobbies and interest. Including hobbies and interests has made many participants want to ask me questions about this, during breaks and has helped to create a better rapport between us.

Where appropriate, I then get each person to introduce the person they interviewed. This tends to cut down the amount of time it takes to get the introduction s completed. Otherwise, if I do not use pairs, I get the individual to tell the class about him/herself, using the headings provided.

Tip: After personal introductions, I find it useful to positively comment of the experiences mentioned by the participants. I then point out that each participant will bring some relevant observations and knowledge to the course. I then urge then to share and listen to others experiences, as this will enhance their understanding.

A starting Exercise (to encourage active participation)

By encouraging your participants to be active at the start of a course, you set the scene for how you are going to conduct the course. The following exercise will give the Participants a sense of ownership. By getting them to work in small groups. You will promote the idea that they will learn from each other, as well as from you.

A useful way to find out what your participants think is important to them is to:

1. Issue each person with a card measuring 6 Inches x 3 Inches (152mm x 76mm) or sticky notes of a similar size.
2. Ask them to write down 3 to 5 things what they want to gain from the course.
3. Tell them they have 10 minutes.

Once you observe that they have finish writing or the 10 minutes have elapsed, then ask for a volunteer to read out their objectives for the course. You can then tell them when or whether this will be covered. If it is not going to be covered, then tell them at this time. It is better to state this clearly at the beginning, rather than the participant find out at the end of the course. They will more likely accept the situation at the introductory session and it will have a less negative effect, than if they find out at the end of the course. You may be able to advice them of another course that may cover this item, or suggest that you may be able to help with this item, outside of the timetable.

Once a participant has finished talking, ask them to post their card/ sticky note on a wall of the classroom and explain that, as you go through the course, you will be visiting each of these cards every day to see how their items are being covered. On following days, or at the end of some sessions, I take a few minutes to review the cards and see if we have covered what people's requirements, to their satisfaction. Every morning, I ask each person to review his/her card stating what has been covered on it and what remains to be dealt with. This exercise shows that you take their learning needs seriously and gets them involved in thinking about the course and what they may be able to get from it.

Whilst this exercise takes a little time, the benefits are excellent, in that it tends to make participants realise that you are interested in what they want to learn. It also gives you information on what the learners think are the important topic on the course. By getting the participants to share what they individually think they 'need to know', it is likely that other participants will realise that they also "need to know ' the same or similar things. (For the value of getting participants realising what they need to know, see "How adults learn')

It may be helpful to you to use a classification that I have been using for a few years, to label the **initial attitude** of course participants.

I classify participants as being:

1. **Learners** – Participants come to the course wanting to learn. They start willing to learn and usually will work hard to do so. You can damage their enthusiasm by using poor training techniques and squash their enthusiasm
2. **Holidaymakers** – These participants come to the course to get away from work (sometimes as a

reward for hard work). They will enjoy the location of the town or city where the course is being held and will like to party and sightsee. Often they will also be willing to put real effort into learning, particularly when they see that the Instruct/ Trainer does not apply rules too rigidly. Most Holidaymakers can be encouraged to learn too, especially if the atmosphere is relaxed in the classroom.

3. **Prisoners** – These participants do not want to be on the course for various reasons. Some will feel they do not need the course and already know all about the course subjects (they are often mistaken about this). Or they feel that they are being 'punished' by their manager, by being sent on the course. Another reason that I am seeing much more these days is that some participants have such a high workload; they feel they do not have time to attend the course and often are expected to complete complex assignments whilst being away from their work place.

The earlier you can identify which group each participant is in, the more effective you may be able to deal with that individual in a positive way. Early identification is important and the more you can ask individuals to talk and interact, the more likely it is that you will be able to determine their individual attitudes. We will be looking at ways of dealing with difficult participants in the chapter entitled **"Dealing with Difficult Participants"**.

Setting the Course Ground Rules

Imposing rules on adults does not always work. A group usually observes rules if they devise them themselves.

This exercise is fairly short:
Get the group members to:

1. Write down a few thoughts about:
   What do I expect?
   Of myself: What am I expecting to put into the course. This helps the individual to realise that they have a responsibility for their own learning.
   Of My Peers: What help and information will I be looking for from other participants? Sometimes individuals realise that what they expect of others they must be prepared to give themselves.
   Of My Trainer/ Instructor: This will often show unrealistic expectations that you can deal with at the debriefing of this exercise. It also allows you to emphasise that you are there to help and answer queries.
2. Ask participants to read out what they have written.
3. Ask them what rules should we have in the Group to ensure that these expectations are achievable.
4. Write down key words that convey the 'rules' on a flipchart. You may need to prompt the group if they have forgotten important issues like the use of Mobile phones, use of computers/tablets during session and time keeping. It allows you to emphasise the importance of time keeping and keeping discussions 'on topic'.
5. By displaying the finished flip chart in a prominent position in the classroom,

you may be able to refer to it, if you find some group members are ignoring some of the rules during the course. You may find this will hep to improve the situation. By reminding participants that they agreed these rules, you are more likely to improve such situations. We will be dealing with how to handle difficult participants and situations later in this book.

Tip: It is useful at this stage to emphasise that participants are responsible for their own learning and that you will do everything you can to assist them achieve the learning goals. Point out that you can only create the opportunity for learning to take place, but you cannot force anyone to learn.

Introducing the Course Time Table

Most people want to know what they will learn on the course. You may have supplied each participant with a course folder. If so, it is likely to contain the course timetable listing the topics to be covered. I usually have a copy of this projected on the screen at the front of the room. When explaining it, I ask the participants to raise their hands for any topic mentioned that is of particular interest to them. I then write the number of people who found the topic of interest, on my paper copy of the programme. This gives me some valuable information. When I have finished reviewing the programme, I then ask which topic is of least interest to individuals. I often ask 'Why is this topic of little interest? " I mark my paper copy with a minus number corresponding to the number of hands raised. This information is very useful in order to allow me to see where the greater emphasis should be place during the course.

You may also ask if the start and finish times are suitable. Often by changing the start and finish times, you may help your participants miss the 'rush hour traffic'.

By showing that you are willing to be flexible, you will usually gain kudos with the class. It is important that you only implement change to the start and finish times if it suits all of the participants. You may find that a 'start-time' change will make it impossible for one or two participants to arrive on time (often due to school 'drop offs'). It such cases, I will not change the start or finish times.

Stages in starting the course

To review what this chapter has covered, I will now list the stages that I think are important:

1. Warmly greet individual participants as they arrive.
2. Get participants to list their objectives for the course
3. Run Personal Introductions exercise
4. Try to identify the Learners, Holidaymakers and Prisoners
5. Get participants to help draw up the ground rules
6. Introduce the time table and get participants to indicate what they find most and least interesting on it
7. Set up the room layout to encourage the most interaction possible

Having read this chapter, it will help you to write down at least three things that you found useful and that you might use when training:

1.

2.

3.

How Adults Learn

Many books have been written about adult learning, this chapter covers a very brief overview of how adults learn, just enough to emphasise the benefits of participant centred learning. It also contains a further reading list for those who may wish to explore this subject further.

In reading this chapter, we hope you achieve the following benefits:

You will be able to: -

1. Explain how adults learn.
2. Explain why it is essential to stimulate effective communication between participants early in a course.
3. Explain why participant centred learning helps keep learners focused.

Why bother with the theory of Adult learning? What is in it for me? These are valid questions that many trainers may be thinking about. I believe an understanding of the theory of adult learning will help instructors and trainers to:

- Consider how to increase their effectiveness in encouraging adults to learn

- Decide the best techniques to use in a given learning situation
- Consider how will the learning delivered improve the participants' effectiveness?

I will deal with the main components of the various theories of adult learning, rather than delve deep in any one of the theories. I hope this will keep this on a more practical level and be more useful for the working trainer

When adults learn effectively, they:

Learn when they feel the need to know additional information or ways to cope with problems or their interest. Adults will put effort into finding out or learning that will help them deal effectively with problems or improve their skills in areas of work or in which they have an interest. Once they have established that they 'need to know' they will invest considerable effort in finding information relating to that subject. One of the first tasks an instructor or trainer needs to do is to help the participants to understand why they might 'need to know' what is being offered or discussed. " Even more potent tools raising the level of awareness of the need to know are real or simulated exercises in which the learners discover for themselves the gaps between where they are now and where they want to be." (1) This gives the instructor or trainer a different function to that of the 'Sage on the Stage'. He/she is more the 'Guide on the Side" who points out possible solutions or places where solutions may be found. He/she may use their experiences as a resource to enhance understanding. Learning becomes a cooperative activity between the learners and the trainer.

One of the most common mistakes subject matter experts make when teaching is to try and cover everything they have learned over their career, during a course. Information overload is counterproductive. Psychologists believe that most people can only absorb between 5 and 9 pieces of new information, at any one time. The ability to absorb information depends on the complexity of information received and the freshness or tiredness of the person receiving the new information. This has serious consequences for instructors and trainers. This is why in face-to-face classes; tutors need to continually scan their participants to monitor signs of fatigue. To combat fatigue, tutors should change activities often and also ensure there are sufficient breaks. Such breaks do not necessarily have to be long – 10/ 15 minutes is usually sufficient to rejuvenate course participants. Many courses have set times for breaks. Whilst this is often necessary for meals, trainers should be flexible as to when most breaks are called. Body language signals and verbal indicators from participants should guide trainers, as to when breaks are necessary.

Adults bring to a course some Knowledge and Experience. Very few adult Learners arrive on a course with absolutely no knowledge of the subjects being delivered. They will bring with them a wide range of individual different experiences, some of which will directly relate to the topic being considered. Adults earn best when they can connect new knowledge with what they already know about the issue being delivered. Their prior knowledge is an essential part of the learning process and that is why it is important to stimulate effective communication between participants as early as possible in a class. By using tasks, techniques and exercises that encourage participants to 'Tap into' their experiences and knowledge, the trainer will add considerably to the learning and to the atmosphere, on the course. " In an adult class the student's experience counts as much as the teacher's knowledge. Both are exchangeable at par. Indeed, in some of the best adult classes it is sometimes difficult to discover who is learning most, the teacher or the students" (2). On every course that I have ever run, I have learned something useful. This is particularly true when I ask participants to share their experiences with the class. For learning to be really effective, it is important that participants are able to link new knowledge to their existing knowledge.

Adults learn by Doing

> I hear, I forget
> I see, I remember
> I do, I understand!

This is an old saying that holds good for a lot of people, and in my experience, most adults appear to want to 'DO'. Why is this? Many adults dislike just sitting and listening to a lecture. They see it as being very much a one-way form of communication. If they know, that following the fairly short lecture, there will be some form of exercise, where they will be expected to use the knowledge and information given in the lecture, then they will be much more likely to pay attention during the subject under consideration. I believe that it is because they wish to try out what they have learned, in a practical, real world situation, to validate the benefits to them, of such information or knowledge or be asked to try out some skill. Trainers should have exercises available, relating to the topic under discussion. Such exercises allow participants to interact with their peers and share existing experiences. By changing the activity (from passive listening to a form of interaction) the trainer will energise the participants and assist learning. Another benefit is that, by using such exercises, you are encouraging learners to reinforce their learning and to help them transfer such learning to long-term memory. By getting participants to 'apply' new knowledge to a practical or work related activity

(even if just simulated in a class exercise), you are using one of the best forms of memory reinforcement.

Another useful way of inspiring adults to learn is the use of '**Guided Discovery**'.

This is where the trainer guides the individual or group to find out the information needed. This tends to ensure that such discovered information is remembered. I believe in the old adage:

> **What I tell you**
> **You forget,**
> **What you find out and tell me,**
> **You remember**

Adults learn best when in a 'Safe Learning Environment'. Adults need to feel respected and have their opinions valued. If they do feel that they are respected, then they are likely to ask questions, comment on what you and others say and challenge anything with which they disagree. By developing a collaborative learning atmosphere, you will help reduce stress, thus allowing more energy to be channelled towards the learning process. "Most people earn better in community than they do in isolation. When everyone in a learning group is a teacher and a learner simultaneously, the stress level goes way down and the learning shoots up" (3)

Who is responsible for creating and maintaining a 'Safe Learning Environment?

This is the responsibility of the instructor or trainer. (The Chapter on "Getting Buy in at the Start' has useful hints and tips on this.) If participants believe that you really care about them and their learning, they are far more likely to make a real effort to maximize their learning. This will require a lot of patience on the instructor or trainers behalf.

Adults like to experience various teaching methods. It has been know for some time that not everyone learns better in the same way. Most individuals have a preferred learning style. They tend to absorb, process, understand and retain information when it is delivered in a way that allows them to employ their favourite learning style. If you agree with this, then it is important that you use a variety of instructional/ training techniques to ensure that you cater for all the likely preferred learning styles of your course participants. Relying on lectures and PowerPoint presentations alone will not exploit the benefits of delivering learning in a variety of ways, in order to cater for the various learning styles. This subject will be dealt more fully in the chapter entitled **"Using Learning Styles to enhance Learning"**, later in this book.

I have only dealt with the main points about adult learning. If this triggers an interest in this subject, I suggest you read some of the work that Malcolm S. Knowles has produced. (There is a reference at the end of this chapter) It is worth reading.

Different types of learners

Not everyone learns in the same way. Most people have a preferred learning preference, although they can learn using their non-preference learning methods, often not as effectively. It is impracticable to test each participant to find out their learning preferences, so trainers and course designers **need to use activities that cover all the main ways people like to learn.**

The major preferences are:

- **Visual learners**

    Visual learners gain most by processing information that they see. They like:

    1. Printed information
    2. Pictures
    3. Graphics
    4. PowerPoint/ Keynote presentations
    5. Posters
    6. Flipcharts
    7. Demonstrations
    8. Workbooks

- **Auditory Learners**
    Auditory learners learn most by hearing. They like:

1. Presentation
2. Lectures
3. Group activities followed by debriefing
4. Question and answer sessions
5. Discussions
6. Group activities
7. Verbal Instructions
8. Demonstrations

- **Kinesthetic**

  Kinesthetic learners prefer the hand-on approach. They like:

  1. Hand –on activity
  2. Individual/ Group activities
  3. Simulations
  4. Producing Flow Charts, maps and models

There are many ways of looking at learning styles. One of the most useful, in my opinion is one devised by two British practitioners, Peter Honey and Alan Mumford. Peter Honey is a chartered psychologist and management consultant and Alan Mumford has been involved with Management training and development.

Their approach to learning styles looks at the motivational side of learning and I have found this extremely useful. They have divided learners in to 4 types of learners and stress that most learners will have a predominant learning style, and will learn using the other learning styles too. They classify their learning styles as:

Activists
Pragmatists
Theorists
Reflectors

Activists like to learn by being active and very much enjoy new experiences. They are willing to trying out things, and like being actively involved. They do not like passive roles.

Pragmatists will look for the practical application of what they are learning or about to learn. They need to see a practical use for what they are being taught. They are keen to experiment. They see themselves as grounded in reality.

Theorists like to be given logical theories. They think problems through in a step-by-step approach. They do not like 'loosing ends' and needing a degree of certainty. They need time to think things through.

Reflectors want to think things through. They tend to listen to others and evaluate what they see and hear. They tend to be cautious. They need time to come to a conclusion.

I have been using this form of learning style classification for many years and found that the major contributors in class tend to be the Activists and Pragmatists, unless I use group work!

Honey and Mumford have developed an individual questionnaire that is easy to use and tells individuals what their learning styles are. It is very useful for instructors and trainers to know too.

I must stress that I have given a very basic explanation here of the Honey and Mumford learning styles. I strongly suggest that you read the Manual of Learning styles by Peter Honey and Alan Mumford. The Learning Styles Helper's Guide, 2009 (4)

Memory and Recall

I believe that we need to look at three types of memory: Short–term, Long-term and Sensory memory. It is important that a trainer considers all three types when it comes to deliver learning.

Short –Term Memory

This form of memory deals with small piece of information and has limitations. We use short-term brain functions to decide the value of the information received and decide what to do with it. The typical human brain can process between 5 and 9 pieces of new information, at any one time. Whether it is 5 or more pieces of information we capture will depend on the complexity of the information and also how tired we might be at the time. This fact might have implication as to how we manage the after lunch training sessions. The use of visual, props, demonstrations may help short-term memory, provided they deal with the subject.

Tip: When conducting an after lunch training session, pay particular attention to body language. If you start to see yawns, participants becoming distracted or fidgeting, then change the activity or call a short break.

Long-term Memory

Long-term memory is the brain's storage system and is used to recall information deemed of value, from the short-term memory. Important information deemed worthy of keeping, by the participants, would be transferred from short-term memory. Memory of emotional events, both pleasant and unpleasant, will also help the transfer into long-term memory. Repetition greatly assists participants to move important information into long-term memory. Examining information, then having an exercise where that information is used, followed by a debriefing session is one way of achieving this effectively.

Sensory Memory

This kind of memory is often triggered by experiences, that are is already stored in long-term memory or prior learning. Trainers, who use phrases in questions that result in praise, may trigger further engagement when participants link the phrase with positive encouragement, whereas a trainer who uses a type of 'put down' may result in participants' memories causing a negative response.

The Value of Repetition

By understanding how memory works, a trainer can create learning sessions to ensure that their participants understand the concepts. Then by employing activities that use the knowledge, allowing the associated skills to be practiced, and using various recall activities, the trainer can ensure that participants transfer the learning to their long-term memory for use after the course has finished. The trainer needs to continually link such learning to previous learning and experience in order to reinforce important points.

Recommended Reading

Malcolm S. Knowles. The Adult Learner, 5th Edition 1998, Gulf Publishing Company, Houston, Texas, USA, ISBN 0-88415-115-8

Harold D. Stolovitch and Erica J. Keeps, Telling Ain't Training 2nd Edition,2011, ASTD Press, ISBN-10: 1-56286-701-6

Roger Buckley and Jim Caple, The Theory & Practice of Training, 2000, Kogan Page Limited, London, UK, ISBN 0 7494 3199 7

Peter Honey and Alan Mumford. The Learning Styles Helper's Guide, 2009 TalentLens, a division of Pearson Education Ltd, London, UK. ISBN 9781902899282

(1) Malcolm S. Knowles. The Adult Learner, P.65, 5th Edition 1998, Gulf Publishing Company, Houston, Texas, USA ISBN 0-88415-115-8

(2) Gessner, R. (ed.). The Democratic man: Selected writings of Edward C Lindeman. P.166. Boston: Beacon, 1956

(3) David Meier, The Accelerated Learning Handbook, P16-17, The McGraw-Hill Companies, Inc. 2000

(4) Peter Honey and Alan Mumford. The Learning Styles Helper's Guide, 2009 TalentLens, a division of Pearson Education Ltd, London, UK. ISBN 9781902899282

Having read this chapter, it will help you to write down at least three things that you found useful and that you might use when training:

1.

2.

3.

Course Design and the importance of measurable Objectives

In reading this chapter, we hope you achieve the following benefits:

You will be able to: -

1. Explain the benefits of measurable learning objectives when designing and delivering training sessions.
2. Explain how measurable training objectives can be used to test whether or not the participants have learned what they need, having completed the session or the course.
3. List ways that measurable objectives can help trainers decide the appropriate methods and content to use in a training session or course.
4. Demonstrate the ability to write measurable learning objectives, listing Performance, Conditions and Standards.
5. Explain the stages in designing a course or training session.

What should be in your course or training session? How do you find out or decide? It is imperative that you consult:

1. End user organisation (They often will be buying the course).
2. Subject Matter Experts (SMEs) in the subject area.
3. Experienced practitioners/operators may highlight important practical aspects to be covered.
4. Potential participants.
5. Awarding bodies, if you wish to get your course accredited.
6. Other training courses dealing with this or similar subjects.
7. Academic papers and books on the subject.

Sometimes you may be commissioned to produce a course by a particular organisation. Some people see training as the answer to every problem and this might not be the case. It is important to be open minded about how problems might be solved and sometimes this will not be by producing a training course.

It is important to take time to ask questions and help the client develop the desired outcome. Once you have established this, you will be in a position to set the learning objectives. Learning objectives will be essential to determine the course content and are essential in establishing how effective the training has been. Learning objectives should be set up in consultation with likely sponsors, so that they can agree that the learning outcomes are what are required. Learning objectives are the measurable learning outcomes you want your participants to be able to demonstrate at the end of the course or session.

Tip: People support what they help to create, so the more **people you consult** during the design phase, the better.

Once you decide to produce a training course (or training session) then you will need to decide on who should attend. You will also need to decide what the entry level of potential participants should be. What basic knowledge and experience will they need, before the start the course?

How many people should you have on the course? Using small group work means that participants are likely to take an active part and become deeply involved in the learning process. Having between 12 and 16 people on a course usually helps to establish and maintain a sharing of knowledge, experiences and expertise. It is easier to maintain a trainer/participant rapport and a relaxed atmosphere. As the numbers increase, then these aspects are harder to maintain. It is almost impossible to have an intimate atmosphere with a class of 36 or more participants.

Other issues you will need to think about are:

1. Is it basic awareness, essential application or for experienced practitioners?
2. Who are the likely participants?
3. How much time will be allowed to complete this training?
4. Do I have sufficient knowledge and experience to design and/or run the course, at the level required?
5. What resources are available to design, produce and deliver the course or learning session?
6. Is there a book I could build the course around?
7. What are the constraints? (Financial Constraints? Time pressures? People to review and give feedback?)

8. What is the expected life of the course or learning session likely to be?

   Tip: When designing your course or learning session set a future realistic review date. This will help keep the course or learning session up to date, otherwise it is likely to become obsolete, almost unnoticed.

It is tempting to include pre course work. This is often suggested to insure that participants come to the course with sufficient entry-level knowledge to ensure that everyone starts at the same basic level. However, I have not had good experiences with this approach. Too often, the pre course material fails to reach the participant, or the participant fails to undertake the pre course learning assignments, due to too much work, family commitments or other reasons. I am therefore reluctant to include this feature in any of my courses. If necessary, I will start a session with a quick review of the basic knowledge needed to be able to cope with the learning offered.

Once you decide that a course or session is needed, you might consider asking three or four colleagues to brainstorm ideas that might be part of the course or session. No doubt, you will end up with multiple ideas. Often trainers try to cram too much into a course or session, almost everything they have learned over their working life. You will never have to time to do this and information overload is a real problem for anyone trying to learn and recall knowledge and application. You need to have sufficient depth to ensure you are not just 'scratching the surface', of the subject. Equally, it is a real mistake just to add material just to fill the time.

Producing Measurable Learning Objectives

Learning objectives may be broken down into two levels, in my view. The levels are **course objectives,** sometimes known as terminal objects (that which should be achieved at the end of the course) and **session objectives,** sometimes known as Sub or Enabling Objectives, which should be achieved at the end of each session. Course objectives are developed first, as they tend to help you decide what sessions you need to achieve each course objective. You then write the Session or sub objectives.

An effective **measurable learning objective** must state clearly what the learners are expected to be able to achieve at the end of the course or training session. Measurable learning objectives use action verbs to describe what you want your participants to be able to do by the end of the course or training session.

The learning objective will describe the **Performance or Behaviour** that they have learned during the course or training session. This **Measurable** learning objective must also contain the **Conditions** under which the learners will demonstrate what they have learned and to what **Standard** they must achieve in order to satisfy that they are competent.

You will need to identify the level of knowledge to be delivered. In Bloom's Taxonomy, there are six levels of learning. Benjamin Bloom produced his taxonomy in 1948, as a set of three ranked lists used to classify educational learning objectives into levels of complexity. Lorin Anderson and David Krathwohl revised Bloom's

Taxonomy, in 2001. It's important to choose the appropriate level of learning, because this directly influences the type of assessment you choose to measure your students' learning.

By having a measurable learning objective, trainers will know:

1. If participants have gained sufficient behaviour, skills and/or knowledge to demonstrate they have achieved the learning outcome required.
2. Effective learning objectives give the trainer exact training goals.
3. Learning objectives make the reviewing and upgrading of a course or session so much easier.
4. They help designers avoid information overload and produce the right extent of training.
5. Well-written objectives show the learners the importance of the subject at the start of the course or training session.
6. If learning objectives are shown at the end of a training session or course, they often remind the participants what they have learned.
7. A learning objective will show if a learning activity is likely to lead to participants being able to demonstrate enough learning to satisfy the measurable learning objective outcomes.

I have often designed a 'fun ' exercise that I thought would be a great learning tool. When I measured it against the learning objective I realised that it did not help participants achieve the learning outcome I had hoped. Learning objectives are a great way to check how effective our course and session design is.

Look at the two following objectives:

"At the end of this chapter trainers will be able to design a learning activity"

When looking at this objective, I can see the performance /behaviour is there, but there is no condition or standard. A participant that designed any learning activity (effective or not) would meet this learning objective. The above objective would not be sufficient to establish whether or not the participant could produce an effective learning activity on a given subject.

Now look at this Learning Objective:

*"Given a training need (**condition**), the participant will be able to design a learning activity (**Standard**) that demonstrates effective learning has taken place pertaining to the subject of the activity (**performance**)"*

Having a **measurable** learning objective, means that we can get a mental picture of what is required when we come to design our learning activities.

When writing Objectives you need to:

1. Use Action Verbs to describe what participants need to be able to do. (See list of verbs below Figure 2)
2. Decide on the level of knowledge that you want your participants to achieve. It is useful to use

Bloom's Taxonomy to achieve this. Bloom lists six levels of learning. By choosing the suitable level of learning, you will see the type of assessment you need to select to measure participants' learning. The Revised 2001 version looks like this (figure 1).

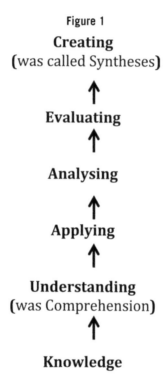

Figure 1

Creating
(was called Syntheses)

↑

Evaluating

↑

Analysing

↑

Applying

↑

Understanding
(was Comprehension)

↑

Knowledge

The lowest level is the knowledge level **Action verb** that helps you construct **Measurable Learning Objectives** shown in the table on the next page.

Figure 2

Knowledge	Understanding (Comprehension)	Applying (Application)	Analysing (Analysis)	Evaluating (Evaluation)	Creating (Synthesis)
Describe	Classify	Apply	Appraise	Appraise	Arrange
Identify	Contrast	Calculate	Analyse	Assess	Assemble
Label	Compare	Change	Arrange	Argue	Compose
Locate	Differentiate	Classify	Calculate	Choose	Construct
Memorise	Discuss	Complete	Classify	Compare	Create
Name	Describe	Discover	Connect	Conclude	Design
Order	Estimate	Employ	Contrast	Decide	Develop
Quote	Indicate	Interpret	Criticise	Discriminate	Formulate
Recognise	Identify	Implement	Differentiate	Defend	Explain
Repeat	Report	Modify	Deconstruct	Estimate	Integrate
State	Summarise	Operate	Examine	Evaluate	Invent
		Produce	Infer	Grade	Make
		Prepare	Order	Justify	Manage
		Solve	Organise	Judge	Modify
		Use	Question	Measure	Organise
			Separate	Predict	Plan
			Select	Prioritise	Prepare
				Prove	Rearrange
				Rate	Rewrite
				Recommend	Set Up
				Select	Substitute
				Summarise	
				Support	
				Test	

If you examine the different categories shown in the above chart, you should be able to decide on what level the objectives should be aimed. Basic courses will tend to use the action verbs, the Knowledge and Understanding columns, where advanced courses will tend to use the action verbs listed in the right hand columns. I find that I often refer to the above chart when I am writing my objectives.

Like any skill, the more you practice at producing learning objectives the better you will become. Try writing a couple of objectives to cover the following areas:

(The answers will be shown at the end of this chapter)

1. If you are intending to run a session on writing objectives and the desired aim is whether or not participants can produce a measurable objective, remember to cover "Performance", "Condition" and Standard.

Write your answer here

2 You are designing a 30 minutes session that covers 3 different types of participant centred learning activities

Write your answer here

Matching Learning activities to your Objectives

Once you have decided on the level of knowledge that you need to deliver and have written your learning objectives, you will now need to decide what learning activities you might employ to enable participants to achieve those objectives.

You might use one or more of these learning activities to help your participants achieve the learning objectives. I have explained some of these activities in more detail later in this session. Some suggestions that are linked to each level that you might consider:

Knowledge: Lectures, "war stories (recounting personal experiences/ practices), Use of Posters, Visual Aids, Video Clips, Examples, Quizzes, and Short Tests. Various hand-outs that give more information on the subjects discussed also help.

Understanding (Comprehension): Diagrams, Discussions, Comparing, Discussing Posters, Producing Summaries, Producing Reports, and Identifying Situations & Components. Discussing Usage.

Applying: Forecasting, Demonstrating, Calculating, Employing, Discovering, Role Playing, Listing, Proposing Questions, Solving Problems, Completing a Project, Producing a Diagram or Flow Chart.

Analysing: Surveying, Completing Problems, Undertaking Exercises, Undertaking Case Studies, Constructing Graphs, Discussing the subject.

Evaluating: Undertaking Case Studies, Carrying out a Self Evaluation, Writing Conclusions, Deconstructing Knowledge or Process or Machinery, Testing a Theory or Machinery or Process, Making Decisions, Making Recommendations, Constructing and conducting Surveys, Completing a Project.

Creating: Creating a problem that others have to solve, completing a report on a Case study, Developing plans, Designing Quizzes or Problems, Producing Explanations of Complex Issues.

Some learning Activities explained further

Lectures/ Presentations. See the Chapter on effective Presentation and delivery for hints and tips on this activity.

War Stories: Use "War Stories" (anecdotes of your practical experiences) to illustrate points you need to emphasise. It is important that you do not use this to brag and such stories **MUST** help to add to the understanding of the subject matter being discussed. I have seen trainers use these stories to try and impress their participants, rather than to add value. This then becomes counter productive.

Posters Sessions: You can use a poster or series of posters to explain something. It is something different from using PowerPoint or a Keynote presentation. Another poster activity I have used is to display the poster and get Groups of participants to list the things they know about the subject shown. Once they have completed this task, they will then be interested in your explanation of the poster. This is another way to gain interest or "buy-in".

DVDs and Videos: The use of Video/ DVD clips can stimulate real interest. Keep the clips short (never more than 12 minutes). and give participants a task when watching the Video or DVD. This ensures that they will pay attention. It is important that you then debrief the task at the end of the clip. You will need to allow time to do this.

Quizzes: This is a great way of reviewing material, particularly after a lecture. Another activity, using small groups is to get each group to devise two or more questions (they must know the answer to the questions they devise). Group 1 then asks group 2 the questions, Group 2 ask group 3 and so forth. The last group asks group 1 the questions. This is a great way of reviewing material. See the section on Kahoot in Chapter 10 for an innovative way to introduce an electronic quiz.

Discussing Usage: After a presentation get groups to list how they might use the information gained. Each group then presents their finding to the whole class.

Identifying Activity: Ask groups to identify situations where the knowledge explained might apply or show the participants a Diagram and get them to identify the various components and explain the purpose of each component (if they can). If they have trouble with any component then the trainer should help them understand that particular component's function.

Producing Reports: Again this is a good small group of exercise. After a lecture on a subject a set of circumstances are given where the participants have to apply the knowledge learned. It is helpful to give them some report headings and stipulate the time for the completion of the exercise.

Calculating: This is particularly useful in engineering and scientific courses, when sizing components or identifying conditions are an issue. By explaining the process and then running through the calculation with the participants, they get a 'feel' for figures generated. It is useful to give the participants another problem where they have to find the values to input and then use the same calculation to achieve a correct answer.

Case Study: This is an activity best run with small groups, that requires participants to practice skills and judgement, working together to solve a problem or situation. The trainer takes a real situation (often from the newspapers) that has some link to what the participants are studying and gets them to analyse the situation and come up with a solution or recommendations. It is a participant centred activity that requires individual thought and group construction of knowledge. This encourages group members to share their experiences. Groups report back in a plenary session. A very powerful tool particularly if debriefed well by the trainer. This kind of activity does take planning and time to run and debrief.

Case Exercise: This is like a mini case study. It is usually written by the trainer or course designer and consists of a scenario that requires the small groups to make decisions about the application of one or two aspects the knowledge studied to a given situation.   This has many of the advantages and disadvantages of the case study.

Demonstration: A Demonstration is an activity, usually carried out by the Trainer (or an Assistant with the trainer commentating) from which the course participants can observe and learn. When used appropriately it can be very effective. Having participants actually doing an activity helps keep interest and often puts the subject of the session into context. (See the chapter on "Training Aids and how to use them" for details of how to conduct a demonstration effectively).

Role Play: This activity allows participants to practice skills whilst playing various roles in order to solve problems or improve their interpersonal skills. It can be effective in the 'soft skills' area. The trainer gives each member of a small group a card containing information about the role to be played. The trainer sets the scene and each player then acts the assigned role. At the end the Trainer then debriefs the exercise. This can be very powerful, but needs careful preparation and supervision.

Tip: As a result of a badly run role-play exercise in the past, I have found some resistance to the use of the term role-play. I have found it easier just to assign roles and start the exercise without using the term Role Play.

When designing a course or constructing a training session, by starting with measurable objectives, a trainer can lay the foundations of an effective course provided the learning objectives are valid. Another advantage of having measurable learning objectives is that they tell potential sponsors, and participants what they will be able to do, or know post course. This material is ideal to include in advertising material when looking for participants. It is important that we know what we are trying to achieve, when we set out to design a course or training session and measurable learning objectives allow us to know where we are heading. It is worth spending time on thinking and then writing the best measurable objectives that we can.

Object Exercise answers

1. By the end of this session (condition), participants will be able to produce a Learning Objectives (performance) that clearly measures the learning outcome (standard).
2. By the end of this 30 minute discussion (condition), you will be able to explain 3 types of learning activity (standard) for delivering participant centered training (performance).

Having read this chapter on Questioning, it will help you to write down at least three things that you found useful and that you might use when Training:

1.

2.

3.

Using Group Work effectively

Whilst reading this chapter, we hope you achieve the following benefits:

You will be able to: -

1. List the advantages of using small groups.
2. List some of the disadvantages of using large groups.
3. Explain why small groups should not have more than 6 members
4. Demonstrate using Groups of 3 to allow participants practice various soft skills.
5. Explain how pairs of participants can assist learning.

Group work is the foundation of participant centred training. I prefer to use small groups, as I have found that such groups tend to get everyone involved. Some of the reasons I believe small groups are an effective way to transfer learning, are:

- Working in Small Groups encourages participants to share their views in a low risk way, particularly if they tend to be shy.
- Small group work encourages peers to exchange experiences and thus learn from one another.
- Participants are very likely to take an active involvement in the various activities.

- Participants are likely to share diverse views, which help with problem solving and the learning process.

Some potential problems:

- Occasionally a trainer may find that one participant does not take an active part in the group to which he/she is assigned.
- A failure to produce an answer or a report to the exercise.

To overcome this, I suggest the following

1. Ensure that each group has selected someone to produce a Flip Chart with bullet points and that they have appointed a speaker and time keeper.
2. Each group is informed that they will have to give input to the whole course, at the end of the exercise.
3. Ensure each group has a Flip Chart pad (and if possible an easel) and Marker Pens.

Obviously participants form a large group prior to learning tasks being started and also when groups report back at the conclusion of an activity. Ideally the total group should not exceed 24 or 25. Having run courses with 36 participants will require much more management by the trainer.

Group Size

In our experience, whilst running exercises when possible, groups should be made up of between 4 and

6 participants where possible. Where small groups of two and three can be effective, having at least 4 participants tends to ensure the groups' actually construct further knowledge and thus increase learning.

Groups or three are very useful (sometimes known as triads) when undertaking exercises where individuals have to try and put theory into practice. One example I can think of is when I asked course participants to experience investigating employee misconduct. I constructed 3 scenarios and then split the course into groups of three. I labelled each person either A, B or C in each group. In the first scenario A became the supervisor, B became the employee and C was the observer. This tested A's ability to ask questions, probe and establish facts. B was able to state how he/she felt about the questions being asked and C learned by observing and having to give feedback. When the second scenario was run B became the Supervisor, C the employee and A was the observer. In the third scenario C became the supervisor, A the employee and B the observer. This allowed everyone the chance to practice using the investigating and feedback skills. Each of the scenarios was written to ensure an aspect of employment law was covered.

Working in pairs (also know as Dyads) can be easy to arrange and usually results in participants actively getting involved with their 'partner'. It is usual for colleagues to sit together on courses, so it is useful to request that participants pair up with someone they do not know. Pairs work well because it is usually non-threatening and people find it easy to build a rapport with their new partner. This is often very useful as an Ice- Breaker during introductions, where one of the pair questions the other (having been given a set of questions) and then introduces that person to the entire group of participants, at the conclusion of the introductory exercise. Pairs can be merged later, in an exercise to form larger groups. This allows pairs to compare answers and thus extend their total knowledge, prior to reporting back to the overall group. Pairs are also useful when participants have to demonstrate practical skills or undertake laboratory tests.

Bigger groups, we have found:

- Encourage one or two people to dominate.
- It is also more difficult to control large groups.
- Participants are more likely to take a passive role in the larger group.
- It is difficult for individuals to build rapport and trust, which is essential for effective learning to take place.
- Non- Subject related conversations (often known as 'side conversations) tend to occur.
- Time keeping is difficult to control because of more input from group members, even if just from a small number of active participants.

Large Group

There are occasions when the trainer will use a large group, typically the whole class. This will often be at the start of a learning session or when debriefing various learning activities. The trainer will often ask questions of the whole group, which results in individual participants giving their thoughts on the issues raised.

This will often result in various participants commenting on what is being said. Using the whole group to debrief a learning activity allows various small groups to report their answers and thus share their finding amongst everyone.

Changing the composition of small groups

By often changing the composition of the small groups on your course you are likely to:

1. Ensure that participants meet many others on the course. This will expose them to different views, experiences and abilities.
2. Moving participants often results in energising such small group members.
3. Circulating members to other groups will help 'brake up' cliques and expose people to members from other organisations or departments.

Seating

Encouraging participants to move into small groups should be as easy as possible, with minimum of disruption. This will depend on the training room layout.

The most advantageous lay out for small group work is the Round table layout (figure 3 in the chapter 'Getting Buy In at the Start').

The next best layout is the Chevron Shape (figure 2 in the chapter 'Getting Buy In at the Start'), where participants can work on each side of the table when undertaking group work.

Similarly, the 'U' shaped layout (figure 2 in the chapter 'Getting Buy In at the Start') can also be used, by asking participants to use both sides off the tables.

The Classroom set up (figure 1 in the chapter 'Getting Buy In at the Start'), is less suitable, but can be used as at a push. If the room is big enough you may have extra tables at the back of the Classroom set up, or break out rooms where participants can go to work in groups.

The lecture theatre set up, is almost impossible to use for group work without having additional 'break out' rooms.

Setting up your Small groups

Tip: Using your business cards (see figure 1.) You can change groups easily. Prepare the cards prior to the start of the training session. Then give participants a card and tell them to keep the card for the duration of the course.

When you want to start an exercise you select either letters, numbers or symbols The first exercise you may decide to select letters: so all the A's make up one group, all the B's in a second Group and so on. In order to change the composition of the groups, for the next exercise may be selected, so all the 1's in one group, all the 2's in another group and so on. You can then change the composition again by getting participants to form groups using the symbols on the cards.

If you do not want to use business cards two changes can be achieved, using playing cards. If you select Aces,

Kings, Queens, Jacks (and maybe 10's), you can get participants who hold the Aces, Kings etc. in groups. You will then mix up the groups by using the various suits, by saying "Everyone with a Heart in One Group, a Spade in another Group and so on. You are limited to 4 groups using playing cards, as there are only 4 suites. This is not so using your business card (or just pieces of card), as you can use more letters numbers and symbols on cards you make up yourself. Have a look at Figure 1

Figure 1 using the back of your business cards to set up small group members

A 1 +	B 2 *	C 3 @	D 4 $
A 2 @	B 1 $	C 4 *	D 3 +
A 3 *	B 4 $	C 1 +	D 2 @
A 4 $	B 3 +	C 2 @	D 1 *

Columns and rows can be added to accommodate more participants. In the past I have used this system successfully, to allocate 36 participants into small groups. One advantage is that the instructor or trainer does not have to do much to change the composition of the small group, once the cards have been issued.

Introducing the Learning Task

When introducing a learning activity, it is vital that the instructions given are precise and clear to the participants. It may be helpful to list a 'step-by-step set of instructions, particularly if the task is complex.

Tip: I found it useful to get a member of one of the groups to repeat back to me the instructions in his/her own words. I do this before participants start the activity and ensure that all the participants can hear what answer I am given. This allows me to correct any misunderstanding.

Ensure instructions are visible to the groups throughout the activity. If you are using break out rooms issue each group with a printed sheet containing the instructions.

Keep the instructions as simple as possible. Instructions should state:

1. The time allowed for the exercise.
2. Material available for use, or required to be used ("Results on a flip Chart Please").
3. The 'Reporting Back "procedure (Bullet points on a Flip Chart, Oral Presentation, Written Report).

4. That the trainer is a resource that can be accessed if the Group gets into difficulty.

Monitoring the work of small groups

The trainer will need to monitor how the groups are working on the task. This is best done as unobtrusively as possible, so as not to inhibit the discussion and activity. By moving around between the groups, the trainer will be able to:

1. Answer any questions that the groups may have about the task

2. By listening to the on going discussions, the trainer may gain some new ideas. or be able to correct misunderstandings.

3. The Trainer will see what progress different groups are making on the assignment.

4. Act as a 'spur' to groups who may not be making maximum effort.

Having read this chapter on Using Group Work Effectively, it will help you to write down at least three things that you found useful and that you might use when training:

1.

2.

3.

Asking effective questions and dealing with Questions to enhance learning

In reading this chapter, we hope you achieve the following benefits:

You will be able to: -

1. Demonstrate how to use the tips given to more effectively answer questions asked.
2. Identify the different types of questions and when they should be asked.
3. Demonstrate the use of the questioning techniques (know as the 4 P's) and the use of silence
4. Explain how the use of silence helps participant engagement.

Improve how you ask questions.

Effective Questioning is a valuable way of gaining information, reinforcing knowledge and determining the motivation (or lack of it) amongst your course participants. The trainer establishes an effective two-way communication process with the trainer asking and answering questions. Questions allow course participants to check their understanding of the subject the trainer has been teaching and can also result in a participant adding further knowledge to what has already been said. Their answers often add a practical dimension to the knowledge being discussed. Tutors add considerable value to any subject when they give examples of how the knowledge at issue is applied in the working environment.

By use of questioning, the trainer can check existing knowledge, what knowledge gaps may exist, check knowledge transference, and challenge and query information brought to the course by participants. An import part of questioning gives the tutor the ability to ascertain if the course actually meets the needs of the participants. An effective question can be used to stimulate a discussion, bring out existing experiences and get course participants to consider how the presented knowledge might be used, in a practical way back in their work places. Questioning may also expose some attitudinal problems that might result in resistance to learning.

It is important to be aware of the fact that some course participants may be reluctant to answer questions in front of others for fear of giving an incorrect answer. Small group work is a useful way of combatting this problem. By asking the question to a number of small groups simultaneously, the quieter individuals are more likely to share their knowledge. With effective debriefing of the small groups, after they had time to discuss the question, the tutor can insure that his/her question has been given serious consideration by everyone.

Professional Instructors and Trainers will engender an atmosphere where course participants feel happy and safe to ask questions and to challenge what the trainer has said. The trainer at the start of the course should introduce such a helpful atmosphere. This is done by:

1. The trainer actively seeking the views of the participants .
2. The trainer giving subtle praise to individuals that contribute their views.
3. Showing respect for all contributions, even when they are incorrect.
4. Correcting incorrect assumptions in a non-threatening way. ("I see where you are coming from. Has anyone else got another answer?").
5. Responding to the questioner by name. Name cards, also known as 'name tents', on desks/ table help with this.

Let us look at answering questions first!

It is important to fully understand what you are being asked.

Some tips that you may find helpful:

1. Listen carefully to what is being asked.
Trainers need to listen with their eyes as well as their ears and give their whole attention to the questioner. Too often tutors allow themselves to get distracted and do not properly hear the question. They then answer the wrong question. The other regular fault is when trainers interrupt the questioner before thy have completed the question. This again, often results in an inadequate answer being given.

2. Repeat back the question asked in your own words

This allows the person asking to question to verify or correct your understanding of the question. Many people, whose first language is not the same as the language used on the course, may have some difficulty of phasing the question correctly. This stratagem allows them to repeat the question using different words, if you have not grasped the meaning of the question they asked. It also allows other participants (with maybe a better grasp of the presenting language) to re phrase the question.

3. By you repeating the question, other participants are guaranteed to hear the question asked.

In a large room or with a large number of people in a class, often many participants do not hear the question asked by another participant. If other participants do not hear the question asked, they often lose interest and cannot add to any answer you might give.

I found it takes time to remember to repeat the question asked. It is very worthwhile doing this and my experience is that course participants really appreciate it too! You will need to practice repeating the question back to your participants. You should review this issue, at the end of each course to see how often you have forgotten to do this. It really is worthwhile.

Participants should feel encouraged to ask questions as this shows that there is interest and that your class are involved. A learning event may even be run as Question and Answer session. Planning these sessions is important and I have seen trainers deliver their whole session by using 'Question and Answer' techniques. They start by using the learning objectives of their session to formulate their questions, thus ensuring they have covered the session's objectives effectively. This often appears to be less formal and stimulates 2-way communication with the learners.

Over time, especially when running the same course, the tutor is likely to be asked the same or similar questions and will have developed effective answers that enlighten the participants. A useful way of handling some questions is to throw the question open to the class, by saying "I know that some of you have particular knowledge of this question? Would you like to answer it before I do?" or "Anyone like to answer Fred?" This gives participants a chance to show their knowledge to their peers. However, **a word of warning!** In some cultures, particularly in the Far East, this may be taken as a sign that the trainer does not know the answer. Another potential problem is when a participant gives an incorrect answer and you then need to ensure that the correct answer is given, without leaving the answering participant feeling silly.

Some instructors and trainers ask the course participants to save their questions until the end of the sessions. This has some advantages:

1. The trainer can concentrate on the lesson
2. Questions may be better thought out or the trainer may answer the question as part of the session later in the presentation.

3. The trainer can prevent extroverted participants from dominating by taking questions from other participants having answered one question from the extroverted individual.

There can be some disadvantages with doing this.

1. The participant may need to understand the concept being given before they can understand an issue being raised later in the session. This is known as a 'Building Block' approach to learning. You need to understand point "A' before you can understand point 'B'.
2. They may forget the point they wanted clarified. This often happens. That is why using a Flip Chart pad (often called "The Parking Lot") to write down the question, the trainer does not fail to remember to answer it later. If you use a "Parking Lot' system, you must review it regularly. Most trainers review this document at either the end of the day or first thing in the morning.
3. Time pressure may result in participants being reluctant to ask questions at the end of the session, particularly if it is just before a break or at the end of the day.

Most questions will be asked in order to clarify a point or to ask for examples. Some questioners will be seeking attention, peer recognition or to further their understanding of an issue. Occasionally, the questioner will ask a question to show his/her knowledge of the subject, or to undermine the tutor. It is important that the tutor remains calm, treats the participants with respect and never verbally attacks the questioner. Otherwise the good will of the class is likely to be lost. Treating hostile questioners with respect will often get the rest of the class to appreciate the trainer's skill and keep the class on the trainer's side. If the hostile questioner persists, peer pressure is likely to make the person desist.

Don'ts's

1. **Do not pretend you know the answer.** If you do not know then admit this, as otherwise you will end up damaging your credibility. You may ask the participants if anyone knows the answer, if they cannot answer the question, then say you will try and find out the answer. Then make every effort to do so.

   Tip: Some trainers use a Flip Chart as a "**Parking Lot**" to list items they need to find out about or to insure that issues raised can be addressed later. This ensures that such issues are not forgotten and many tutors review the class "Parking Lot" at the beginning or end of the day. Being part of an online Trainer network may help a great deal, in these situations, as you can email the network to try and get a quick answer.

2. **If the question is outside the reference of the session, do not just dismiss this question.** You should point out that this course does not cover this aspect. You may try and find out how many

others are interested in the issue raised. If there are a few then maybe you can find time to deal with the issue. If it appears to be only the questioner who is interest, offer to discuss it on a one-to-one basis during a break. In my experience most participants do not take up that offer. If a participant does, you will find that he/she will really appreciate the time and effort you devoted to help that individual.

3. **Occasionally, someone may strongly contradict the trainer. The trainer must not argue**. It may be helpful to ask the person for supporting evidence to back up their point. Do not allow an argument to develop. I have defused such issues by saying" I think we will have to agree to differ on this issue" and leave it at that.

4. **Do not interrupt someone who interrupts you.** Stop talking and let the person finish what he is saying. Say, "Thanks for that question/ comment. I will just finish what I was dealing with and what I was saying and will come back to your point when I have finished".

5. **Never use Sarcasm.** It is very tempting to be sarcastic when a participant asks a question that has been asked a short time before. It could be that the participant was distracted, when you dealt with this question previously. It may be that the participant just did not understand the answer you gave. It may be useful for you to answer the question in a slightly different way.

Coping with participants who fail to understand

Occasionally a trainer will face a participant who, despite the trainer's best efforts, fails to understand a concept or point. This can be real challenge to any trainer. He/she needs to be careful not to 'leak' a superior body language that may be seen, as the him/her thinking the participant is stupid.

Some suggestions to help this situation may be:

1. Asking supplementary questions about each element of the misunderstood concept to establish where the learning blockage is.
2. Show patience and consideration, as the participant is likely to feel a bit depressed, because of their failure to grasp the concept.
3. Remember it is the trainer's failure to communicate effectively enough, not the participant's failure to understand that is the issue.
4. If the trainer believes that the participant can achieve the necessary understanding, this will be reflected in the trainer's Body Language and tone of Voice. This information will be subliminally transmitted to the participant.
5. If pushed for time, offer to meet with the participant during a break or after class to re-visit the issue, in order to help the participant get over this learning hurdle.

Why should you ask questions during Class?

There are a number of valid reasons why you should ask questions when running any training session. Some of them that you may not have considered are:

1. Questioning promotes two-way communication.
2. Questioning keeps participants mentally active.
3. Questioning allows you to assess how much of what you said has been understood.
4. Effective Questioning permits you to detect and correct misunderstanding.
5. Questioning asked effectively should be a real aid to reinforcement.
6. Questioning allows participants to link what you are teaching with their experience, especially if you ask them how they might use this knowledge.
7. It allows you to use your experience to link theoretical knowledge to practical application when you expand on answers given.
8. It can promote interest in the subject being taught at the start of a learning session. And example of this is: "Why do we need to know this?" or "What benefit might the knowledge on this subject have for you? The answers given to such questions often highlight benefits that no one person had considered.
9. It permits you to see where the knowledge gaps are that you must deal with.
10. Questioning permits you to see how relevant the participants appreciate the content of the session meets their needs.

It is important to use **brevity** when asking questions; Long-winded questions result in participants becoming confused or becoming bored. They must be **relevant** to the issue being discussed. **Avoid the use of multifaceted questions** (or Multiple Questions), as participants will not know what answer to concentrate on. **Make**

participants think by using questions that will enable them to consider the issue being discussed.

Do not forget the non-verbal types of encouragement that helps when people start to answer questions. This are: Smiles and nods of the head. Para-language also helps. This is the "Uh', "Huh?" "I understand" or "I see.

We can break down questions into various type and such types can be used to achieve different results.

Let us consider some of the most useful types of questions that can be employed by trainers to enhance their training sessions.

OPEN Question.

The most commonly used type of question is the **OPEN Question.**

This cannot be answered by a yes/ no answer and the answerer usually has to explain in more than a single word answer.

Open questions usually contain one of **the 5WH** words. They are:

Why, What, Where, When, Who and How.

An Example of an open question is:

"What benefits might the knowledge of listening skills be to you in your work?"

This kind of question is very useful when exploring knowledge and gathering information. In some instances, if phrased correctly, it can also be used effectively to encourage your class to starting thinking about any subject you are about to teach. An example of this might be: "What benefit might you obtain from knowing about {Subject of the lesson}?" This often gets participants to realise the importance of the subject about to be taught.

An Open question is **NOT** useful when dealing with a verbose participant or where there is conflict or emotional energy in your class, on the subject being discussed.

CLOSED Question.

This is very useful for probing a single fact or for concluding a discussion. This type of question is useful to bring a discussion back to the point at issue, if asked correctly. It usually requires a yes/no or very short answer. Often useful to prevent a participant digressing, when that is not helpful.

An example of this type of closed question is

"Do you use the benefits of listening skill in your job?"

This is not the type of question you would ask if you wanted to promote or expand a discussion, although you might ask supplementary question to probe the answer given. Which brings us to the next type of question.

PROBING Question

A Probing Question is used to expand an answer or to the check a fact.

If it is to be used effectively, it is vital that the Trainer listens to the answers given prior to forming the probing question or selects some fact the class has received.

Examples of a probing questing is:

"When you say you use listening skills in you job, can you tell me how to do this please?" "What do you mean, when you said …..?" "Tell me more about …?"

Having asked a probing question and having listened to the answer, the trainer can pursue a particular part of the answer given, by asking another probing question. An example of this is that if the answer received from the previous question is "It is important to encourage the speaker so that you improve their delivery. "You might follow this up by asking," What methods would you use to achieve this?"

TIP: If the trainer wants to extract the maximum benefit from a discussion on a subject or issue, then the trainer uses **the QA QA system.** This stands for Question – Answer -Posing another Question formulated from the answer given, and then asking it. This process may be repeated until the Trainer is satisfied that the issue has been fully explored.

A word of warning! If the discussion becomes heated, then suspend the asking of probing questions, the trainer can often defuse the situation by bring the discussion to a close, using a closed question.

REFLECTIVE Question

This type of question, if formulated correctly, will get the participants to thinking about the issues involved. The 4P's tip (See 'The 4 P's" later in this chapter) is very useful, particularly when asking a reflective question.

It is vital that the trainer gives participants the time to think about their answers.

An example of a reflective question might be "Think about a time you became aware you were being encouraged to talk, what techniques did the person use to do this"? **Remember give people time to think about their answers.** Reflective questions may also be use to ask participants to reflect on why they hold certain views. An example of this use of a reflective question might be" When you say that this system is useless, can you give me the reasons why you have formed that conclusion?"

HYPOTHETICAL Question

This kind of question poses a hypothetical situation linked to the situation under discussion and if phased correctly will get participants to think about how they might apply newly acquired knowledge to a practical situation. An Example might be "Just imagine you have a very shy person talking about their experience, what things might you do to encourage them to continue to talk?"

It is important that the hypothetical situation described in the question is realistic.

LEADING Question

This type of question can be used to reinforce information given previously and to gain agreement about an issue. An example of this type of question might be " I expect you all agree that encouraging others to speak helps you listen more effectively?" It should be used sparingly, because a trainer should try and promote discussion and reflection.

MULTIPLE Questions

A multiple question or questions are a number of questions asked at the same time. Such form of questioning is **not effective because the participants are unsure of which question to ask.** An example of this might be "How many ways are there to actively listen, when should you use them and when should you not use them?

Knowing the different types of question and when to use them is an important skill for any instructor/trainer. Effective use and handling of questions is important when assisting people to learn. Vary the type of questions you ask regularly.

Too many trainers ask a question and then answer it themselves. Practice the use of silence after you have asked a question. You will be surprised how often someone in the class will volunteer an answer. This is because, for many people, silence makes them feel uncomfortable.

Tip: There is no point asking questions unless you really listen to the answers. Too many trainers spend the time thinking about their next question rather than listening to the answers given.

The 4 P's

How you ask a question is as important as what kind of question you ask. The 4 p system is worth perfecting.

It will take a little practice to become second nature to you

Propose the Question. To not pre-nominate a member of the class to answer the question ("John, name a few ways of active listening?"). By not nominating someone when asking the question, others in the class are likely to consider an answer to your question ("Name a few ways of active listening?")

Pause. This permits participants time to consider their answer. During this pause, you should be scanning the class looking at participant's body language, and who is showing keenness to answer your question. This pause does not have to be long, just a few seconds.

TIP: The use of silence is a very valuable technique when asking questions. When posing questions, it is important that you use your eyes, to see who may be keen to answer the question, who may be bored and who may seem reluctant to answer. You can then make a choice as to who you wish to answer the question. Do not be afraid to allow the silence to continue for many seconds. The wait will appear longer than it is, so you need to show patience. This will, more often than not, result in one of the group making an attempt to answer. It is surprising just how hard silence is to bear. In the unlikely event that nobody answers you have two choices: You can re phrase the question or you can give an answer yourself, asking if anyone was thinking along the lines of your answer.

Pick. Having considered the body language of the participants, you should then select a person to answer the question. Never risk asking a question that may result in the person being embarrassed. Paying attention to body language will help you prevent this.

Praise. Once the person has given an answer, you must acknowledge his/her effort, even if the answer is incorrect. Why? Well, we all like to be acknowledged and valued. By doing so you are setting up the 'Safe learning environment' where participants will feel safe to answer question, even when they are unsure. Be careful not to over do the praise. "Yes. Correct. A good answer" or "I like the way you explained that". If a person answers a question incorrectly, show him/her that you valued their efforts. "Thank for that. It is not really what I was looking for. Anyone else like to answer this?" Or "I can see how you are thinking. It is not quite what I was looking for. Can anyone else help here?"

An important part of questioning is developing active listening (see the chapter on 'Listening Skills') so that you fully understand questions that are asked and answers that are given.

Simple answers are more effective than complex answers and should be used where possible. It is important to allow participants time to consider their answers and trainers should use that time to study the body language of the participants, as this will give the trainer some idea of who is keen, who is confused and who is reluctant to answer. Trainers must refrain from answering the question they ask themselves, unless after a prolonged pause the participants fail to offer an answer and if this happens the trainer should try again by rephrasing the question. Only then if no answer is forthcoming should the trainer give the answer, otherwise participants will be tempted to let the trainer answer all the questions, which defeats the purpose of Questioning.

Too many trainers fail to allow enough time for participants to think and then answer a question. Many trainers end up answering their own questions, without allowing their participants time to think and answer.

Questioning is a valuable skill that improves with use provided the trainer reflects regularly on how he/she is asking and answering questions. Questions are a great way to find out how successful you are at transferring knowledge and sometimes skills. It allows the instructor/ trainer to see when participants misunderstand something. It is also a great way to review and recall the important issues contained in a training session, provided the trainer has given some thought to the questions to ask, prior to the session. Such questions should be designed to test that the learning objectives have been met.

Tip: Ask small groups to formulate questions on a flip chart, at the end of your learning session, they then can ask another group the questions they have formulated. The process of formulating the question is an effective reflective practice. Having them then ask another group those questions and answering other groups' questions, is an effective way to reinforce key points of the session.

Tip: Get groups to develop 5 Key learning points. These are points that members of the group considered very important to their learning and understanding of the subject. When each group presents their answers, you can then ask questions to get them to expand on some of the key learning points. This is another great way to reinforce learning.

Having read this chapter on Questioning, it will help you to write down at least three things that you found useful and that you might use when Training:

1.

2.

3.

Getting the most from Debriefing

Whilst reading this chapter, we hope you achieve the following benefits:

You will be able to: -

Explain why debriefing is important.

Explain the possible effects of feedback on the individual.

Explain what debriefing is.

Explain how to debrief effectively.

Exercises and learning activities

Learning activities and exercises, on courses are popular with participants because it is a break from just listening to the trainer. If such activities are designed properly they can link the knowledge being taught with actual work place practices and in some instances, actually develop skills by allowing the participants to practice what has been taught. However, too many trainers run activities and then fail to debrief the activity or debrief the activity badly. An effective debrief of a learning activity will add learning and reinforce knowledge already gained during the exercise or session. It also allows the trainer to correct misunderstandings and helps participants share current knowledge and experiences.

Benefits of debriefing Learning activities/ exercises

By debriefing the exercises and most other non-trainer led learning activities, the trainer takes the opportunity to get the groups to revisit the learning activity in a structured way. This allows the trainer to expand and revisit the learning outcomes of the activity. Exercises and most participant centred learning activities encourages the course participants to engage with other members of their group to share their experiences that relate to the subject at issue. They also have the opportunity to share their individual understanding of what the sessions are about. The trainer effectively debriefing the exercise or learning activity allows the various groups to share their findings. Each group may produce slightly different answers to the exercise and by debriefing; this allows everyone to see what others have concluded. The debriefing allows time for reflection of the subject under study and reinforces the learning, in probably the most effective way. An effective debriefing session should confirm whether or not the participants have successfully grasped the learning objectives of the training session.

Effective debriefing also allows the trainer to enable the participants to build on their own experiences and to correct any misunderstandings. This only happens when the trainer asks effective questions linked to the issues being dealt with. The debriefing process gives the trainer an ideal opportunity to encourage participants to share 'real life experiences' linked to matter under study. When this happens, it invariably links the learning to 'real life' processes and usually results in the participants understanding how they might use the knowledge gained in their work place. This is much more likely to result in participants transferring the knowledge learned to the work places.

The debriefing activity appeals to all learning styles provided it is carried out skilfully. Well-run debriefing sessions are an excellent and enjoyable way to reinforce learning and often allow course participants to see how the knowledge may be utilised to improve their working ability. This type of activity helps to put the knowledge under study into long-term memory.

Feedback

Feedback is an important tool used by a trainer to appraise individuals and groups about their performance. Giving constructive feedback to groups at the conclusion of exercises and activities increases the learning of the groups and is a tremendous way of reinforcing the knowledge connected with the activity. Constructive feedback, if delivered effectively, increases learning, encourages development and increases individual self-awareness. Constructive feedback will, on occasions, include giving corrective feedback. Giving corrective feedback requires the trainer to be sensitive; otherwise the recipients will mentally reject such feedback.

It is important that feedback is seen as balanced and fair. Ensure that the feedback contains positive aspects areas, as well as areas that need to be improved. You need to be able to 'evidence' the feedback by using what you saw and heard. You need to be able to give advice on how you think the participants could improve. Just concentrating on the positive aspects of feedback means that the participants will think there is nothing that can be improved. It is important to concentrate on what the participants did or achieved, not on their individual personalities. Giving feedback to a small group often takes the sting away from a particular individual, when the result is not perfect and yet all of the group can learn from any mistakes made.

When evaluating the results of exercises or reports, think about:

- Did the individual or group follow the briefing correctly?
- Were their results clear, logical and correct?
- Did they show that they had tackled the issues in a way that discovery/learning took place?
- Did they produce a logical conclusion?
- Did it appear that everyone in the group contributed? ?
- Did they come up with alternative possible answers?
- Did they keep to time?

5 Ways of Giving Feedback

Having thought about the various ways of giving feedback, I have come to the conclusion that I can identify 5 ways. I consider only one to be effective. My grading of the types of feedback are as follows:

1. **Personal and Judgemental Feedback:** "*You are stupid*" This kind of feedback (Exaggerated I know and hopefully never used by a trainer – only used to illustrate the extreme) attacks the individual's self esteem and does nothing to improve the learning.

2. **Judgemental Feedback:** "*The Group's work is poor, you entirely missed the point!*" This feedback does not attack the personalities, but it risks damaging the individual team members' egos and does nothing to improve the learning.

3. **Limited Feedback:** "*Your answers to the exercise was fairly clear, but unconvincing*" The trainer has given limited information, but failed to give any helpful information to allow the participants to correct or improve their performance.

4. **Limited Questioning Feedback:** "*How well did you complete the exercise*" This gets the group to consider how they completed the exercise, but it needs more questions to be effective

5. **Developmental feedback:** "*What were the main learning points of this exercise for your group?*" "*What else did you consider?*" "*How will you use this information in future*"? These questions get the group members to think about the issues involved. This feedback does not contain any judgemental element and I would expect the trainer to consider the answers and give subtle praise where justified.

Giving feedback

1. **It helps to start with a positive aspect.** It is very important that the recipients of feedback actually listen to the feedback give and that they take seriously. If you launch into negative aspects of their work, they are likely to switch off. Most people need some encouragement to stay engaged and by showing that you valued some of their work, constructive suggestions are more likely to be accepted and acted upon.
2. **Specify exactly what you saw or heard.** Tell the individual or group exactly what you saw or heard, and why you valued it or considered it needed improving.
3. **When giving Constructive feedback give suggestions as to how improvements might be made.**
4. **Use 'I' Statements:** This shows that you are not afraid to "own' the feedback. "I saw", "I consider" or "I feel" make more impact than just saying "You did this!"
5. **Give the recipients some control.** To lessen the chances of resistance, offers alternatives, so that the participants can make their own decisions.

Possible effects of feedback on the individual

It is useful for trainers to understand the possible psychological reaction to constructive feedback, particularly when not given effectively. It is easily to accept positive feedback, although it may be embarrassing at times. Constructive feedback can cause some form of distress.

All feedback will affect different people individually, in different ways. This is influenced by how the individual perceives the feedback. Even slightly negative feedback can be construed as a 'Personal Attack". Poorly delivered feedback is much more likely to cause this reaction and real care needs to be taken when giving feedback. The Mnemonic SARA is useful to remembering some of the effects that constructive feedback can cause. Dr Barbara Annis, who is an expert on Gender Intelligence, suggests that men and women routinely move through these stages at different speeds, conducted research.

Possible Psychological Effects of Giving Feedback

The effect start with:

Shock: This is caused to the individual who has not performed as well as we expected. This may result in that person becoming resentful. They may think or even say, "Who the hell are you to tell me off anyway".

This often leads to:

Anger: The individual is often angry for making the mistake, or for not reaching   the standard required. Sometimes the individual will show the anger to the person giving the feedback. Comments like   "I don't have to take this from you!" or "Just you wait until you get something wrong? "It can make the individual want to extract some form of revenge.   Often the anger is directed inwards, at themselves. "How could I have been so stupid"?

Most people actually get through the anger stage very quickly and often without making any remarks, they then get to the constructive stage of:

Realisation: The individual starts to seriously consider their own performance and how they reacted to the feedback.

This then leads to:

Acceptance – The individual now realises that they have room for improvement. At this stage, the individual starts to take on the development suggestions.

Too often the individual can get stuck in the ANGER stage. They can only move forward when they have completed the 'Realisation' and 'Acceptance' Stage.

I think it is worth explaining this process briefly on courses, because once everyone understand it, they tend to move more quickly to the acceptance stage. This makes the job of giving and receiving feedback so much easier. Trainers need to select their words carefully when giving feedback. It is a major skill of any professional trainer.

Group Size

In our experience, when running exercises, groups should be made up of between 4 and 6 participants where possible. Bigger groups, we have found, encourage one or two people to dominate. Where small groups of two and three can be effective, by having at least four participants, this tends to ensure the group actually construct further knowledge and thus increase learning.

Effective debriefing

We consider a debriefing to be effective when it: -

Is delivered in a planned way.

Is flexible.

Encourages reflection and the sharing of experiences.

Gets participants to consider how they would use the ideas in the work place later.

How to debrief effectively – the 3-Stage system

When carrying out the debriefing of an exercise or learning activity, it is vital that the trainer uses skilled questioning techniques (See the Chapter "**Using Questions to enhance learning**"). It is vital to get active involvement from the course participants and it is essential that the trainer employ effective listening skills too (see Chapter 9).

I suggest trainers use the following system, when debriefing any activity.

The trainer should cover the following stages when conducting a debriefing of an exercise or learning activity. The system is three "Whats? "

1. "What?"

It is usual to start with questions like:
"What did you consider was the cause?'
or
"What happened?"

This stage is important because by asking the groups to explain what they saw as the issues, the whole class gets to understand what issues were considered and what problems were identified. It also allows for participants to express their feelings and reactions to what they are considering. Feeling and reactions will affect their judgement. You should allow the participants to share their feelings about what they saw, heard or read. Do not rush this stage. Ensure you listen fully to what is being said. This will allow you to correct any misunderstandings of the facts of the scenario and also to understand where the group are coming from, in relation to this scenario. This stage needs to be properly debriefed, if the process is going to work effectively.

2. "So What?"

This stage usually starts with questions like:
"So what was the result of this happening?"
"What caused this to happen?"
"Why was this a problem?"
or
"What lesson might we learn from this?"

This stage forces the participants to draw conclusions from the circumstances studied. It helps to link the activity to their experience and the experience of the trainer and, if conducted effectively, should underline the importance of knowledge being studied. This stage will usually show up misunderstandings that some of the participants may hold. Such questions should identify any mistakes made by the participants during their discussions and what mistakes the participants, when studying the facts at issue, uncovered. When debriefing of this stage is conducted effectively, it will help participants gain a greater understanding of the issues and help to keep them motivated too.

3. "What Now?"

This stage usually starts with questions like:
"How will you use this information in your job?"
"As a result of what you have found out, what will you change when dealing with similar issues in the future?"
or
"Will this cause you to change how you do things in the future"

This stage of the debriefing should get the course participants to consider how they might include the knowledge learned in their future work. It encourages them to link the knowledge under study to their past experiences. From this third stage, participants can use the answers in the post course action plans, if they decide to produce an action plan for the future. Such action plans should include important learning points they have gained from the course.

Powerful Learning Tool

By including exercises and participant centred activities, trainers cater for all learning styles, especially when they debrief such activities effectively. You will notice that the all the questions listed above in the 3-stage process, are **Open** or **Probing** questions. This is because such questions encourage the participants to think about their answers.

When Designing Exercises and Learning Activities

When designing exercises or learning activities, trainer should keep the 3-stage debriefing process in mind. It is useful, at the design stage, to formulate suitable questions to ask at each stage of the 3-stage process. For new courses, it may be wise to prepare prompt cards to assist you when running such debriefing sessions.

Tip: When you have run the same exercise a number of times, you may start to find the same mistakes arising, (always good for learning) or the same questions. It is useful to makes notes of these and keep them with the Exercise brief. This way you can develop good responses even before the class begins.

Closed questions can be used to get participants to end a discussion, or to drag them back to the subjects at issue, if they stray from those in their discussions.

Practice

Like any skill, asking and answering questions effectively will benefit from practice and use. This is also true for the skill of debriefing. It is vital that trainers conducting such sessions continually scan the body language of the participants in order to detect boredom and tiredness.

Remember, the 3-stage question system

This revolves around asking three questions based on:

1. "What?"

2. "So What?"

3. "What now?"

Examples based on these ideas have been shown earlier in this chapter.

Having read this chapter on debriefing, it will help you to write down at least three things that you found useful and that you might use when training:

1.

2.

3.

Effective Presentation and Delivery

In reading this chapter, we hope you achieve the following benefits:

You will be able to: -

1. Explain the advantages of using lecturing techniques.
2. Explain the disadvantages of using lecturing as a teaching aid.
3. Produce an effective presentation or lecture.
4. Produce easy to use presenter notes.
5. List ways of making a lecture or presentation interactive.
6. List ways of delivering the presentation effectively.

The ability to deliver a lecture effectively is an essential skill for any trainer, and will need to be employed. Unless there is some form of interactivity, very little of the lecture will be remembered. Unfortunately, whilst personality and charisma are important elements of a presenter's effectiveness, practice will make a real difference. Presenting is a skill and like any skill, regular practice and critical review of one's performance will improve that skill. Peer review can be very helpful too and I strongly encourage trainers to permit their peers to review their presentations.

Advantages

1. New concepts can be explained to the whole group.
2. A lecturette can be effective in clarifying misunderstandings.
3. Can be effective in delivering 'updates' to existing knowledge on subjects.
4. Can be used to highlight features of equipment, software programs or policy changes.
5. May be seen as a welcome change in a classroom activity.
6. The trainer has control over the sequence and content of the material.
7. Some participants like lectures and learn effectively from exposure to them (many do not).
8. One trainer can deliver to a large number of participants.

Disadvantages

1. It is usually a passive learning activity unless used with other activities _ (see Tips).
2. It is a one-way communication medium.
3. It requires highly skilled speakers to prevent boredom and disengagement.
4. Large groups often inhibit questions being asked during or after lectures, other than by the more extravert participants.
5. Large groups often leave individuals feeling 'lost' or not important.
6. Retention of information is very low and recall after 24 hours is doubtful.

7. Not useful when trying to teach or enhance skills.
8. *"What I tell you, you forget – What you find out and tell me, you remember"*. Lectures do not allow for this.
9. The mind can only absorb as much as the seat can endure.

Producing an effective Lecture

You will need to:

1. Know your subject very well. Use Libraries, Subject Matter, Experts, and the Internet. Consult your client base, in order to address the level you need to train. You need to build on what the participant already knows.
2. Know your audience. Who are they, what do they want and why are they attending? Show the participants that you have taken the time to get to know something about their background and needs. (See **Tip 1**)
3. Check your facts before you deliver your lecture and update your lecture when needed. The Internet may be a useful source to do this.
4. The title of the Session can help create interest, so think about it carefully. Make sure the title reflects the content of the session; otherwise you will have some disgruntled participants.
5. Explain the objectives of your lecture clearly at the start.
6. Know your material. This is vital. Review it if you have not delivered it for a long time.

7. Do exercises so you see the "pitfalls' and make the exercises work. This is particularly important where exercises have numerical calculations.

8. *"Tell them what you are going to tell them, Tell them this, And then tell them what you have told them"* (in the conclusion) This will help them remember what you say.

9. Decide how broad or detailed your content will be. This will depend on the knowledge level of your participants.

10. How much time have you to deliver your Training session? (See **Tip 3**)

11. Ensure that your appearance does not distract from your presentation. In some cultures male presenters are expected to wear a suit, shirt and tie. If in doubt, then I always wear a tie, which I can remove if I find that is acceptable. Women should ensure their arms are covered when presenting to the more conservative cultures.

12. Make the best of the venue by adding posters, welcome notices and ensure that water and soft drinks available for the participants.

13. Explain abbreviations (even the most obvious ones – non-native language speakers may have different abbreviations) the first time you use them. Do not assume that all of the participants will know them.

14. Vary the tone and loudness of your voice when delivering your lecture. Monotone speaking will 'switch off ' listeners very quickly.

15. Get 'Buy in' by emphasising the benefits that listeners will achieve (see Tip: 1).

16. Have effective notes (see below) so that you can easily deliver your lecture in a methodical way and can resume effortlessly, if you are interrupted.

17. Do not read from your notes, unless you are using a quote, giving a numerical value, quoting a scientific or legal law or where total accuracy is vital. Written language and spoken language are different and reading from your notes is likely to sound dull.

18. Actively display positive body language (eye contact, open stance and some movement).

19. Watch the body language of your audience. Look for fidgeting, facial features displaying a lack of understanding and signs of boredom.

20. Show enthusiasm (in the use of voice and body language). If you fail to show enthusiasm, why should anyone else show interest?

21. Do not talk too quickly (especially if you have some non-native speakers in your audience). They often need a short time to interpret what you have said.

22. Use pauses to allow the participants to process the information you have given.

23. Clearly state when you will answer questions this will be during the talk or at the end (See Chapter on "Asking effective questions and dealing with Questions to enhance learning").

24. Encourage people to ask questions. By doing so, you will get feedback on how effective your talk was or is going.

25. Use visual aids when ever possible. The best is often the actual object, then a photograph or

diagram. Cartoons can also be useful. By doing so you will give something else for the audience on which to focus.

26. Include Personal experiences that help to explain points and link those points to practical applications. Such examples are often known as "War Stories" (**See Tip: 5:** below).

27. Your conclusion should elucidate the important points of your lecture. (See **Tip 6:** Below)

28. Even if you agree to answer questions during your lecture, you should also leave time for questions at the end. I find when people have enjoyed the lecture; they often think of additional questions or wish to make comments.

When asked a question that you cannot answer, admit this, as otherwise you will end up damaging your credibility. You may ask the participants if anyone knows the answer, if they cannot answer the question, then say you will try and find out the answer. Then make every effort to do so.

Some trainers use a Flip Chart as a **"Parking Lot"** to list items they need to find out about or to insure that issues raised can be addressed later. This insures that such issues are not forgotten and many tutors review the class "Parking Lot" at the beginning or end of the day. Being part of an online Trainer network helps a great deal, in these situations, as you can email the network to try and get a quick answer.

Tip 1: You can get 'buy-in' at the start of your talk by asking the audience some of the following questions:

"Why do you think a knowledge of this subject is important?"

"What benefits is X likely to have, in your opinion?"

"What do you hope to gain from this talk?"

By asking a question like this, you will help to establish a rapport with the group. This sets the expectation that you want an interactive session and may well help to generate and maintain interest. It may allow you to see where you should concentrate your emphasis, during the lecture.

Tip 2: Give the participants a task at the start of the presentation. An example might be "During this presentation, I want you to think about how many kinds of machinery are being referred to and how effective they are being used? "This may well help participants concentrate.

Tip 3: When considering the time and content, consider using the "**Must**", "**Should**", and "**Could**" approach. By using objectives you will know the minimum amount of material you will need to achieve those learning Objectives – the "Must" list should be delivered within the time frame allotted. However, often you will find that the participants are so knowledgeable, that you can 'Stretch them a little by using some material you have prepared in your "**Should**" list. Rarely, you will come across a group of participants who are so quick and/or knowledgeable that they get all of the "**Must**' and the "**Should**' material so quickly that you need additional material on the topic to keep them engaged. This material I label the **"Could"** list. Often you will have a mixed group and when working small group exercises you can give a highly preforming group additional supplementary exercises from, the "Should" or "Could' list.

Tip 4: Develop questions to ask the participants during your presentation. This will give you an indication as to how well the participants understand your lecture and help prevent boredom. Even participants with very little knowledge of the subject will still be able to use their limited experience to give an answer.

Tip 5: Use "War Stories" (anecdotes of your practical experiences) to illustrate points you need to emphasise. It is important that you do not use this to brag and such stories **MUST** help to add to the understanding of the subject matter being discussed. I have seen trainers use these stories to try and impress their participants, rather than to add value. This then becomes counter productive.

Tip 6: At the end of your talk, ask the participants to write down one or two things that they have learned during the talk. This enables people to mentally review what they have heard. Then ask a few volunteers to share their thoughts with the whole group. The answers will give you a lot of feedback about how effective you have been as well.

Presentational/ Lecture Notes

When using PowerPoint or Keynote for presentations, often trainers will use the slides in these presentations as his/her notes. Similarly, if you do not use an electronic slide presentation, and there is good reason not to do so, as such presentations have been over used in recent years, you will need to have some form of notes to keep you on track.

Notes should:

1. Be easy to read.
2. Possible to read from a distance (this allows you to move about and not get stuck behind a podium).
3. Contain figures, facts and quotes that you will need to articulate correctly.
4. Show what visual aids are required and when they should be introduced.
5. Easy to locate where you are at in the lecture. This is especially important when you get interrupted.

Note preparation

This is linked very strongly to research and checking your facts. I find that producing a mind map (see Figure 1)

A very simple mind map I used for writing this section

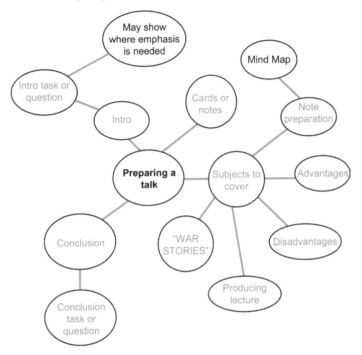

It is a great way to start constructing your talk. Mind mapping is useful to capture your thoughts and then clearly see where the links to the various thought are best made. Mind mapping is non linier and thus allows you to see what is important and also maybe what is missing

Start with the subject in the centre of a blank piece of paper (or use some Mind Mapping Software to construct your mind map). Draw a ring around it. Then other thoughts or sub-headings should be added to the page further out and a line drawn linked to the central topic.

You should use a different colour of text for each new level. You might then see links between these secondary thoughts, so draw a line linking them. You can then add further thoughts further out on the diagram. The beauty of this system is that your thoughts do not have to be in any order. This kind of diagram is easy to read and allows you to see what needs to be included and what maybe omitted. I suggest you try producing a mind map when either writing an assignment or prior to preparing a lecture.

Once you are happy that you have included the entire heading on your mind map, you can now decide what order to talk about the various issues shown. You may decide to omit some that are less important. This may be for time reasons or because people can only absorb so much. Many Psychologists believe that we can only take in between 5 and 9 new pieces of information at any one time. The number depends on the complexity of the information and also how tired a person is who is trying to absorb information. I like Albert Einstein's quote on this too *"It is better my students fully understand half of what I want them to know, than half understand all of it"*

Now you need to produce your notes

You have a choice; you can use Index cards, or A.4 Paper (in the UK) or Letter Size (in the North America).

Using Index cards is one useful way to hold your notes. The most common size for index cards in UK and North America is **3 by 5 inches** (76.2 by **127.0 mm**). Some people call these cards, 3-by-5 cards.

Use one card for each topic. Use a Felt Tip Marker to write the bullet Point about 1 Inch (2 cm) high in a dark colour. The rest of the card can be used for facts and quotes and the bottom of the card for any Visual Aid that helps illustrate the topic (see Figure 2)

Figure 2

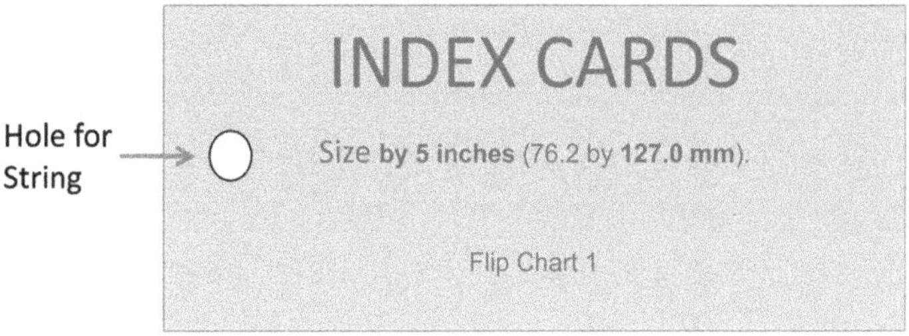

INDEX CARDS

Hole for String

Size by 5 inches (76.2 by 127.0 mm).

Flip Chart 1

Tip: Too often I have seen presenters who use Index cards for their notes, drop them accidently. They then have to scramble to get them back in order. To prevent this, they should put a hole in the left top of the card and thread a piece of string or treasury tag through it. A treasury tag is an item of stationery used to fasten sheets of paper together. It consists of a short length of string, with metal or plastic crosspieces at each end.

Using A. 4 or Letter Size paper for notes. This is the medium I use for my notes when giving a presentation or running a training session. I divide the sheet into 3 columns. (See Figure 3)

Figure 3

Topic	Data/ Quote	Visual Aid
Question	"What Benefits?"	None
Memory	5 to 9 Items	Slide 30
Overload	" It is better that the student fully understands half of what I want him to know, than half understand all of what I want me to know" Albert Einstein	Slide 32
Feedback	Think about the effect on Jack	Video Clip 1
Question	"How to you select which topics to Present?" (5 Minutes)	

The columns are labelled: **Topic, Data/Quote** and **Visual Aid**. I use a Felt Tip Marker to write the bullet Point about 1 Inch (2 cm) high in a dark colour, in the first column, marked topic. The next column can be used for facts and quotes that I may need to refer to or read, in order to ensure I give the correct information. The last column is used to ensure I use any visual aids that might apply to the issues I am talking about.

Tip 1: By using a different colour for each topic, I am able to place my notes on a table or desk and move around. Having the different colours helps me to be able to keep track of where I am in the notes, even at a fair distance. This helps prevent being tied to a podium or lectern.

Tip 2: When you have more than 1 sheet of paper (surprisingly, this is not too often for me!) To prevent the sheets getting out of the correct order, put a hole in the left top each page and thread a piece of string or treasury tag through it. A treasury tag is an item of stationery used to fasten sheets of paper together. It consists of a short length of string, with metal or plastic crosspieces at each end.

Tip 3: Use your notes to schedule breaks for you to ask questions. This way you will tend to keep participants interested. You should have these questioning sessions scheduled every for 10 to 15 minutes during your talk.

When giving a lecture or talk during a training session, it is very useful to start by introducing the reasons why you are undertaking the lecture. As effective learning objectives should state clearly what the learners are expected to be able to achieve at the end lecture, this is a useful way to show participants why they should pay attention, in order to gain something useful from the lecture. Starting your lecture with an explanation of the Objectives of the lecture can be useful, particularly if you have already asked the questions shown in **Tip 1** above.

It is important that you stick to time and finish when you talk was advertised to finish, as members of your audience may have other matters to attend to and will become irritated if they are not released on time.

It can be useful to revisit the objectives that you have given at the start of your talk and ask" *Did I give sufficient information for you to achieve these objectives?*" This should be part of you conclusion. You should also restate the main key points of your talk. Make sure you leave sufficient time for questions from the participants. In the unlikely event of the participants asking too few questions, you should have a few questions that you can ask the participants. These questions should reinforce the key learning points given during the lecture. Avery useful question to ask to stimulate discussion is "*What use can you make of this information when you return to work?*"

In the unlikely event of you having few questions and time available, you might ask your participants to write down the 3 most important things they gained from the session. You can then ask volunteers to give the class some of their key learning points.

Having read this chapter, it will help you to write down at least three things that you found useful and that you might use when training:

1.

2.

3.

Body Language

In reading this chapter, we hope you achieve the following benefits:

You will be able to: -

1. Explain why understanding the effect of body language is important to any practicing trainer.
2. Explain how the 'Fidget Factor' can help trainers determine when to call breaks to be most effective in knowledge transfer.

Studying Body Language

The study of body language is not all that new. An early pioneer of this was Charles Darwin who published his work, The Expressions of Emotions in Man and Animals in 1872. Then in the 1950s, Albert Mehrabian conducted various experiments on communication processes and concluded that information was received by use of verbal words 7% of the time. By vocal means including inflection and tone of voice and paralanguage (ums, ahs and such) about 37% and astonishingly by people reading non-verbal clues 55% of the time. (1) Other researchers have come up with similar figures. Yet as trainers how much importance do we give do our own body language or our ability to read the body language of our course participants? (2)

Why is Body Language important in Training?

It has long been known that much of the communication process takes place by the use of gestures, facial expression, posture position and distance. Physical appearance and body language give us clear clues as to a person's personality without him/her ever having to speak. Yet in training, many trainers fail to consciously recognise either their course participants' body language, or the effects of their own posture, gestures, facial expressions and distance from their participants on the effectiveness of the training being delivered. How often have you seen a speaker carry on speaking when the audience has their heads down and their arms crossed, with no idea that he has lost them?

Body language, facial expression, posture, and dress help people form opinions of a person's personality. Some researchers have found evidence suggesting that people sometimes rely too much on body language and dress over actual information. Even when provided with information about the trainer's knowledge and skill, course participants still rely on body language and dress, when making initial judgments about trainer's abilities as Subject Matter Expert and as an educator.

It is probable that most people subconsciously take some account of the body language being displayed by others, but rarely consider the effects of their own body language on how their communication is being perceived. Culture plays a part in how people display and read body language as well and we will look at this aspect in more detail later.

When a person subconsciously takes account of the body language being displayed, it is often referred to 'gut Feeling' or 'intuition'. Like any skill, reading body language correctly, improves when that skill is practiced regularly. It has been known for some time that women with young children tend to be more effective at reading body language than most others. This is often referred to as 'female intuition'. Very young children lack the ability to verbally communicate sufficiently, so mothers tend to compensate by interpreting the child's body language. Men in the caring professions seem to be better at reading body language than other men as well. The assumption is that having to rely on body language signals for at least some of the communication process improves the skills of these mothers and people in caring professions.

If one accepts that practicing reading body language is effective, then trainers should consciously work on their own body language and on their ability to read the body language of their course participants. In consciously studying the body language of others, you will become much more consciously aware of your own body language and the effects this has on others with whom you communicate. People watching, at social functions, airports and other places where people have to wait or where they tend to spend time relaxing, is a valuable source for improving your ability to read body language.

It is a mistake to think that one can accurately interpret a solitary body language gesture. One should look for clusters of gestures, posture, vocal tones and facial expressions when trying to accurately interpret any meaning using body language. It is also very useful to compare the body language signals with any verbal comment. Do they compliment each other? If not, then most people will rely more on the body language signals to be true.

Tip: When reading body language, always look for clusters of signals and compare any verbal comment to the body language signals. This is likely to give you a more accurate reading of the person's state of mind

Is it easy to fake Body Language?

This is extremely hard to do. Faking one body language gesture is easy enough to do (Open handed – "I am honest" gesture), but to match all the other body language and a verbal signal, at the same time is extremely hard to do successfully. Even well trained people, who try and look honest, sincere and open, can only mimic the body language signals for a short time, if they are pretending to have these traits. This is why you must look for cluster of body language signals, when trying to read how people feel.

What advantage to Trainers?

For trainers being able to discern when their Class participants are:

* Interested
* Bored
* Tired
* Not understanding
* Not agreeing

is essential and being a skilled practitioner in reading body language will greatly help in being able to do this. The trainer's own body language can also display these negative emotions and this will have an effect on their participants. It important that trainers consider how their own body language is viewed by their participants.

Your Body Language

It is recognised that most people decide immediately whether they like a person as soon as they first meet immediately, even before that person speaks. In doing so, they consider:

Dress
Deportment
Facial expressions
and
Gestures

Widely different cultures seem to display the same facial gesture, which seems to suggest that such gestures are inborn. If you accept that initial evaluation of you takes seconds, then you either start on a plus if you leave a favourable impression or a negative, if people do not like what they see. So it is important, that you work on your initial meeting and how you display your body language.

The Importance of 'First Impressions'

Greeting is often the first form of communication when you meet others. If you want your course to start well, the impression you first give will influence this. With everything that one has to do to get the course ready, it is so easy to forget about the image you are displaying.

Researchers have calculated that it takes just one-tenth of a second for us to judge someone and make a first impression. They also found that the more time participants are given to form that impression, the more they believe that impression is likely to be correct. This suggests that the trainer should make time available to carry out what I call the '**Greeting Process**".

The Greeting Process

Be available to greet participants and answer questions before the time the class is due to start. I suggest 20 to 30 minutes should be sufficient. That means your classroom should be ready 20 or 30 minutes before the course is due to start.

Your participants, who you are probably meeting for the first time, are not interested in your "good excuse" for running late. By being available and willing to greet each person as they arrive, you are showing them that:

1. You are keen and enthusiastic
2. You are making the effort to establish an early relationship
3. You are interested in them and their learning.

Your body language and appearance are very important. Physical appearance will help to determine whether or not someone sees you in a positive or negative light.

Your appearance is usually the first clue he or she uses, often subconsciously, to start evaluating you. As Conn Iggulden wrote *"Show them interest, Show them fascination, and they see themselves reflected – and then they will move the world for you."* [3]

Make sure you have an open posture and offer to shake hands in welcome (unless the participant is a Muslim woman, in which case wait until she offers her hand to you!). If you do not shake the hand of a person, a small nod of the head will show that you are glad to meet that person. When trying to create rapport, using a handshake it is advisable to not use more pressure than the other person offers, when they respond to your handshake.

Many people subconsciously "mirror' the actions of people they meet and with whom they have started to build a rapport. This subconscious mimicry seems to suggest that people in a discussion or meeting have similar feelings and thoughts. Although strangers rarely 'mirror', a trainer wishing to develop a quick rapport, might mirror one or two gestures used by a participant when they first meet. Be careful though, too much overt 'mirroring' is likely to cause discomfort and is not helpful.

Remember to smile too. Smiling is contagious and it is likely that your participant will return your smile too. Smiling appears to directly influence other people in a positive way and this is important to you and your course, especially when you first meet your participants. Regular smiling helps to improve relationships and too many trainers fail to capitalize on this. If you appear calm and confident, the other person will feel more at ease, and should result in you conveying a good 'First Impression".

When chatting at this time, introduce yourself, using the name you would like to be called and ask them for their name, and where there are from "Did you have a good journey?" "Where are you staying?' "You do not need to ask too many questions at this time as you will find out more when the course starts. You may also have a number of people arriving at the same time and will therefore have to limit the time you spend with each person. I find it useful to say something like "I look forward to getting to know you better in the next few days, and finding out what you wish to know about..."

When Presenting and Facilitating.

It is vital that you show enthusiasm when facilitating or presenting a session in class. If you as the trainer or instructor are not seen as being enthusiastic, then how can you expect your course participants to be keen to learn? Words alone will never convey your enthusiasm. So what body language do you need to display? What would make you think the trainer was enthusiastic?

Your non-verbal signals communicate your feelings and your message to your participants, so taking care with how you appear is important. Researchers have found that smiling is infectious, even if the smile is not genuine. So starting your session with a **smile** is helpful.

The **tone of voice** you use implies your attitude to the message. Observation after you speak, of your participants' body language, will show how your message has been received. Remember that your tone of voice can come across as aggressive, nervous, critical or monotonous. You should aim for your tone to sound friendly.

Your **body posture** also conveys to the observer your emotional state. When you are in a slouched position, you may appear as being very relaxed or even not keen or enthusiastic. If your posture is too erect, you may be seen as being authoritarian, so an open stance will usual convey an enthusiastic attitude on your part. . Remember too that having your legs crossed or arms folded, may convey a degree of formality or relaxation. Your body posture will effect how your and you message is received.

Body Gestures must be considered too. Almost everyone uses hand movements to confirm, express or emphasize oral messages. Such gestures can convey passion, interest or a dismissive attitude. Over use can distract strongly from the ability of the listener to concentrate on the message. Be careful of some hand signals such as the "V for victory sign (two fingers), as in the UK is consider vulgar, if used with your palm facing you. The 'Zero' shape make with fingers, which in the USA is used to indicate OK, but in South America is considered very vulgar.

Tip: The use of a pointed finger, by trainers are often seen as the trainer being aggressive or rude, and does seem to distract from the retention of information by participants. Using an open hand gesture instead is likely to be more effective.

Eye Contact allows people to see that you wish to communicate, at least non-verbally. It is very much a two way process. Too much eye contact is often perceived as a threat or a person being ill mannered. Too many trainers either use too little eye contact or fail to actually see the body language clues that their participants' are displaying. Using eye contact during a training session permits a trainer to gage the current interest being displayed by the participants. It may also show a lack of understanding by individuals or the wish of an individual to challenge a statement or ask a question.

Tip: When wishing to promote discussion, particularly when you have the whole course together, sit down and carry on the opening of any discussion. This action seems to have a subliminal effective of putting many people at ease. I have found that this helps to promote active dialogue.

Use **the pause** to enhance your delivery. A useful technique, when starting a session, is to stand in silence in front of your participants. This often conveys an aura of authority. I found that it also gets the participants to stop doing what they are doing and prepare themselves for the session to start. Many experienced speakers use the pause effectively. Pausing periodically allows the participants time to think about what is being said. This is especially important for those participants whose first language is not that in which the subject is being delivered, as they often have to convert the words into their native language. If you are delivering new concepts or dealing with complex issue, the pause allows people to "catch up," and to let the meaning of what has been said, sink in. Ex US President Obama regularly used the pause to good effect in this way.

When posing a question, it is important to pause immediately after asking the question. This allows the participants to think about possible answers and provided you do not pre nominate a person to answer, permits you to scan the body language of the participants, and select a person to answer, based on positive non-verbal signals.

Watch for the **fidget factor.** What is the fidget factor? When people get tired or bored, they start to fidget, that is: move in their seats, scratch, yawn, or start to move things around on their desks. Another boredom indicator is when you notice participants starting to support their heads with their hands. This is often an attempt to avoid falling asleep. A single occurrence is not something to worry about, but if a number of people are observed doing so, you should consider calling a short break or changing the activity. Even getting the class to stand and turn around has worked well on occasions for me. Many experienced trainers look for and take account of the **fidget factor**. Not doing so risks losing the mental participation of some or all of their participants.

To sum up using body language effectively when presenting:

- Start with a smile and show you mean it!
- Consider your tone of voice.
- Attend to your own body posture – try leaning forward slightly.
- Use gestures carefully – avoid finger pointing.

- Pay attention to your eye contact and those of the participants.
- Use the pause to gain maximum effect.
- Be conscious of personal space and try and gauge how much space others are comfortable with.
- Actively watch for the Fidget Factor.

Like any skill, reading body language improves with practice. Just being aware of the effects of body language will help trainers look for signs displayed by their participants and thus see when breaks are needed, when understanding and misunderstanding is occurring and when the trainers' own words or body language is having an effect (both positive and negative) on their participants. Most people have little conscious understanding of body language. By being aware of the effects of body language trainers will start to look for, and become conscious of, the body language signals displayed by others.

Most people subconsciously, use and read body language to some extent. However, it has been recognized for some time that by consciously paying attention to your own body language and that of your participants, you will gain far more benefit from this important skill. Communication is the key for trainers.

References:

(1) Mehrabian, A., Silent Messages, Wadsworth, Belmont, California (1971)
(2) Birdwhistell, R. L., The language of the body: the natural environment of words' in A. Silverstein,

(ed.0, Human Communication: theoretical Explorations (203-220), Lawrence, Hillsdale, NJ (1974)

(3) Iggu, C., Dunsten, Penguin Random House UK (2017) P.67 ISBN 978-0-718-18144-4

Having read this chapter, it will help you to write down at least three things that you found useful and that you might use when training:

1.

2.

3.

Listening Skills

In reading this chapter, we hope you achieve the following benefits:

You will be able to: -

1. Explain ways to actively listen.
2. Explain the importance of active listening when conducting a training session or course.
3. List the barriers to effective listening.

Listening skills are an essential part of a trainer's toolbox. The ability to really hear what participants are saying during a training session is essential. You need to be aware of your ability (or lack of it) if you want to improve this important skill. We have already established that having two-way communication in our learning sessions is necessary and desirable. Real communication requires that all concerned actively listen. Trainers can introduce activities that make participants more likely to actively listen, as we will see later in this chapter.

It is important to remember that communication is more than words spoken. Often the speaker is also expressing feelings and non-verbal signals can give a strong indication of the emotions behind the spoken words. Feeling, such as enthusiasm, boredom or a lack of understanding, are usually easy to detect, in facial expressions, stance and hand gestures. Non-verbal clues will either confirm or contradict the verbal message.

Listening is more than the physical activity of hearing. Hearing is done with the ears, whereas listening is done with the brain and the ears. Listening is emotional and intellectual processes that incorporate the physical aspect of hearing. Without thoughtful attention to what is being said, trainers will not be an active listener. **Effective listening has to be an active process**.

Benefits of listening effectively

By improving your listening skills you will gain the following benefits:

- Your participants will tend to trust you more, as effective listeners are considered "good people".
- Improves any relationship you have already developed.
- You will clarify information more quickly.
- You will more easily diffuse emotional situations.

To effectively listen the trainer needs to play an active role in the interchange that takes place with the participants. This activity should help develop understand and meaning about what the speaker is saying.

Some Ways to actively listen are:

1. The trainer needs to know what the participant is saying and why.

2. The trainer suspends judgement about what the participant is saying

3. Concentrate on the speaker and avoid distractions.

4. The trainer should pause before making a response. This helps the trainer interpret what is said and allows the trainer to 'fill in' what is not being said.

5. The trainer asks for clarification or for the speaker to elaborate.

6. The trainer tries to understand the feelings of the speaker said.

7. The trainer should rephrase what the speaker in his/her own words said. This is particularly important when the speaker is not a native speaker and may have had difficulty in phrasing his original contribution.

8. It is important that the trainer listens for the real meaning of what is being said and not just listening to the words.

9. Concentrate on the speaker and what he/she is saying, rather than thinking about the next step.

10. The trainer needs to show positive Body Language. That will include:

   - Looking at the speaker.
   - Displaying an open posture (no folded arms or legs).
   - Using Para language (Encouraging noises: 'I see" "Ah ha" "Yes").
   - Appearing Relaxed.
   - Smiling rather than frowning.
   - Maintain eye contact.

These actions show the participant that you are interested and are listening intently to what they are saying. Body Language gestures are the key to this.

Tip: Never assume that what is first said by the speaker is all they are going to say. If you do you may well miss their real intention in making a contribution.

How do you get your Participants to Actively listen?

In order for participants to actively listen you need to give them a purpose or benefit for doing so. Some of the things you might consider are:

1. Use bullet points rather than sentences on your PowerPoint or keynote slides and on your flipcharts. Written language and spoken language are different and by having just bullet points, you will focus on the subject and explain it in spoken language. This tends to connect more easily that reading the written word.

2. Use the 'reveal' function for each bullet point and only reveal it when you want to speak about it, when showing electronic presentations. Humans are curious and they will tend to 'read ahead' on any slide you display. They then will make assumptions about what you are going to say about bullet points displayed lower down. If they believe they know the subject well (and they may not) they will tend not to listen properly to what you are saying.

3. Give the participants a task at the start of the presentation or video clip. An example might be "During this video, I want you to think about how many times the manager asked his staff questions about the incident shown? "This may well help participants concentrate.

4. If a discussion starts ' blank' the slide (Control B in PowerPoint blanks a slide and use that key again will "un Blank' the presentation) so that the speaker and listeners do not get distracted.

5. Change the activity or participants' focus often to keep interest.

6. Watch the participants' body language for signs of tiredness and call a break or change the activity. Tiredness inhibits effective listening.

There are four main types of listening and trainers should attempt to use all of them and ask their participants to do so as well. They are:

- Informational (Listening to gain information). The trainer can help with this type of listening by suggesting that the participants develop at least 3 key learning point during the session

- Critical Listening (This is where the listener uses logic, facts and evidence to come to a decision). The Trainer can ask the participants for their experiences that might add further evidence to the issues being taught.

- Appreciative (The listener likes what he/she is hearing and is 'captivated'). The trainer may help with this kind of listening by trying to eliminate external distractions.

- Empathic Listening (This is where the listener uses understanding of other feelings, even when disagreeing with what is being said). This is the most difficult of listening skills to master and takes conscious practice to achieve. The Trainer will help in this situation by:

  1. Repeating back what the trainer has heard, in his/her own words
  2. Avoid making judgemental or critical comments.

The trainer may begin listening in an informational mode, but because of what is said, may move into another listening mode. The listening mode used will depend on the situation.

Bad Listening Signs

Trainers should look for some of the signs often displayed by poor listeners. Some of the things a trainer might notice are:

- Interrupting inappropriately. This listener will interrupt regularly and often on subjects not related to what is being discussed.
- Arguing without hearing all the facts. This listener appears to look for opportunity to argue and disagree with the trainer and/or others. Some disagreement can be helpful and should be tolerated, but persistent disagreement will damage the learning environment.
- Taking the conversation 'Off Topic'.

- Being negative about other's ideas. This listener is superlative at 'squashing' other people's ideas. Anything new or different and he readily retorts, "It'll never work" or "We've tried that before".
- Having closed mined. This listener argues or disagrees but that he will take a stand on an issue and will rarely budge from it.
- Trying to dominate the conversation. This listener shows enthusiasm and offers inputs that are not directly connected with the matter in hand.
- Showing disinterest. This listener seems to be doing other work, reading a newspaper or reading emails during the training session. He is not being disruptive.

There are many strategies to deal with bad listeners and I give many tips as to ways to counteract the effects these participants may have in Chapter 11. Dealing with Difficult participants.

By trainers improving their listening skills, they will improve their effectiveness as trainers. It really is worth making the effort to do so.

Having read this chapter on Questioning, it will help you to write down at least three things that you found useful and that you might use when Training:

1.

2.

3.

Training Aids and how to use them

In reading this chapter, I hope you will achieve the following benefits:

You will be able to: -

1. List a number of aids that assist you to deliver learning .
2. List ways of using Slide Presentations effectively.
3. Explain ways of using Flip Charts effectively.
4. Explain what benefits poster may bring to learning.
5. Explain how to keep participants engaged during training sessions using various training aids.
6. List advantages and disadvantages of using training aids.

In this chapter, I hope to pass on many hints and tips, gathered over many years of training, with government organisations, universities and industrial companies. I have trained quite a number of Instructors and Trainers and coached some very experienced people over the years. I found that often such people gave me as many hints and tips as I gave them. I am grateful to them for doing so and this proves the adage that: "*If you want to learn something well, go teach it*!"

I am going to start with the use of **Computer Slide Presentations** (such as PowerPoint and Keynote), as this form of aid seems to have the widest usage at present.

Advantages:

It is relatively easy to construct

If designed effectively, this will allow you to 'stay on track'.

Can be seen by many people, if the right size font is used.

Enables the audience to see pictures and diagrams of what you are talking about at the click of your electronic presenting tool.

Can be re-used from course to course.

Can easily be updated and amended.

May be used instead of Lecturer's notes.

Using a remote device for changing slides allows the presenter to move around and not get stuck behind a lectern.

Disadvantages:

"Death by PowerPoint".

Boring if presenter just reads from the Slides.

Boring if there are no questions or activities during the presentation.

Failing to look at the participants during the presentation makes it impersonal.

(Although you can use this form of presentation and look at your audience).

Technology can and does break down. You need to plan an alternative if this happens. Computer and projector bulbs do sometimes fail to work. Do you know where there is a spare bulb? Do you have Presentation notes if your computer malfunctions?

Tip: Have a back up plan if the equipment fails and cannot be repaired rapidly. Do you have a set of training notes you can use if your computer or digital projector fails.? Do you have photographs to hand around? Trainers should plan for equipment failure, before it happens.

Some Good Practice when constructing a slide show:

1. **Use bullet points** rather than sentences on your slide.

    Written language and spoken language are different and by having just bullet points, you will focus on the subject and explain it in spoken language. This tends to connect more easily that reading the written word. You will come across as knowledgeable. It is often difficult for humans to do two things well at the same time (such as listening and reading). By having just bullet points on your slide, your participants will tend to listen to your explanation of the bullet point.

2. **Use the 'reveal' function** for each bullet point and only reveal it when you want to speak about it.

Humans are curious and they will tend to 'read ahead' on any slide you display. They then will make assumptions about what you are going to say about bullet points displayed lower down. If they believe they know the subject well (and they may not) they will tend to 'switch off'.

3. **Rules for content of Slides.** The following should be considered as useful guidelines (to be broken occasionally).

    Do Use: Pictures, Cartoons & Photographs. This appeals to your visual learners. A picture can be worth a thousand words and can allow your audience to connect with your explanation of the graphic being displayed.

    Tip: You need to pause after displaying a picture, cartoon or diagram to allow the participants to scan the graphic. This allows them to start processing the information on the graphic.

    Use the same design of the slides throughout your presentation. That means you using the same font, colour and size. Position the text in the same place on your slides and avoid using the very bottom of your slide.

    The learning objectives should be shown at the beginning and the end of your session. Showing them at the end allows you to reinforce the important learning points of the presentation. When displaying them it is useful to ask questions and get the participants to state what they considered were their important key learning points.

Tip: Remember: Check your spelling and also any facts or quotes used, after completion of slide show.

Make sure the lighting in the room is not so bright that it makes the slide presentation difficult to see. Too many trainers forget to check this. Sunshine can also be detrimental to your participants seeing the details on your presentation and as the sun moves you may end up with a problem later in the day, depending on the position of windows and curtains in your training location.

Tip: Give the participants a task at the start of the presentation. An example might be "During this presentation, I want you to think about how many kinds of machinery are being referred to and how effective they are being used? "This may well help participants concentrate.

Do not:

Use more than 5 words per line (this is only a rough guideline)

Use 5 lines per slide. To many words or images on a slide makes them 'busy' and difficult for participants to concentrate on.

Use fancy "fly-ins" (A reveal function that makes the words appear very fast from different sides of the slide. Maybe this is 'attractive' the first time someone sees it, but often becomes irritating).

10. **Read from the slide.** This prevents you looking at your participants and tends to make your voice stilted and sounds unwelcoming. If you use Keywords rather than sentences, you will sound much more natural when you explain the keyword.

    Tip: By positioning your computer / laptop between you and your participants, you will be able to see the same slide on your computer that is being displayed on the screen and you will be facing your audience. This way you can see their reactions and body language.

11. **Use a Font size NOT less than 20 point.** Anything smaller will be difficult to see if the venue is large. If you are likely to have lots of people present then increase the font size to at least 24 points.

12. **Do not use a plain white Background.** A plain white background can, over a period, have a slight irritating effect on peoples' eyes, especially when changing from one slide to another.

13. **Use multiple colours.** Try and avoid dark lettering, as this can be difficult to see.

14. **Keep the number of slides to a minimum.** Large slide presentations will result in the likelihood of "death by PowerPoint".

    Tip: If you have more than 10 slides, then ensure you break up your presentation with questions, exercises and promote discussion on some points.

15. **Do not leave a slide on show for too long.** If a keyword promotes discussion, or you start an exercise then ' blank' the slide (Control B in PowerPoint blanks a slide and using that key again will "un Blank' the presentation).

16. **Do not display diagrams that are two small.** It is good practice to either display a diagram that covers the whole of the slide. An alternative is to have the diagram available on a flip chart or in the course manual. Using the flip chart forces the audience to look at something else, as does asking people to look at the diagram in their manuals.

    Tip: If I use the manual then I will have a slide that just has "**Turn to Page XX in the manual to see Diagram 20**" There is no excuse, in my opinion, for the trainer to say "I know you cannot see this very clearly, but it shows...." If it cannot be seen clearly it should not be in the slideshow.

17. **If you give 'hand-outs'** of your slide presentation, print them in black and white rather than using colour. Make sure the handouts are readable, as sometimes they do not print out as well as they appear on the screen.

This is an example of a slide I use (see next page) . You will see I added a page number the bottom left hand corner. This corresponds to a handout or course manual page that I am discussing. You will also see I have not used a white background, as this is more restful on the eyes.

Having read this section, it will help you to write down at least three things that you found useful and that you might use when training:

1.

2.

3.

Lecture Notes Please read the chapter on 'Effective Presentation and Delivery".

Diagrams. These can be very effective, especially when displayed on walls of the classroom, from the start of the course. They will often cause interest and some participants will look forward to having the trainer explain them.

Tip: By exposing the participants to such diagrams (shown on posters or Flip Charts) ahead of time, I have found that a lot more questions are asked about them when I come to use them. It is particularly important to use colours, especially if explaining information on material flows. I have found that, just by displaying a diagram at the start of the course, participants seem to remember the diagram, even before it has been formally discussed.

Pictures and Photographs. It is always better to have these in colour. You may display them via a computer and Digital projector. The advantage of this is that all of the audience can see them at the same time. The other way is to have a number of the same pictures or photographs and split up your participants into groups.

Tip; You can then ask each group to examine the images and then comment on what they have gain from such visual aids. This promotes discussion and helps keep interest.

Tip: If you have a diagram or picture on your computer, you can 'trace' it onto a poster or flip chart by using a digital projector to shine the image onto the flip chart page or poster. By using the flip chart or poster material as your screen, it makes it much easier to copy the image.

Posters. I have found that displaying posters relating to the subject I am presenting, has a very beneficial effect. I am continually amazed how much information course participants absorb, from just seeing posters in the classroom. Politicians have been using posters to influence their votes for years and continue to do so, because it is effective. When you think of it, political parties having been using posters to influence voters for a long time. They have realised that a poster can make a real difference. In training, I think we may have underestimated just how useful they can be, in transferring knowledge and for kick starting discussions too.

TIP: You might consider displaying posters at an angle rather than square on. This often gets participants to notice them initially. Masking tape is often useful for affixing them and rarely does damage to painted surfaces.

Flip charts:

Using Flip Charts (large pads of paper often plain, although lined and graph paper are also available) helps to break up the monotony of just staring at Screens. Flip Chart sheets are very useful for groups to report and display their findings after exercises. Using flip chart sheets is also very useful to display agreements about classroom rules and activities during the course. Remember to have rolls of masking tape to affix completed sheets to walls. As well as having a Flip

Chart Easel at the front of the class, it is useful to have enough of such easels that each group has one to work with.

Flip charts can be 'pre-prepared' by the trainer prior to a class. Make sure the writing on the flip chart is big enough to see from anywhere in the room. I suggest letters should be about 2 inches or 5 centimetres and the writing is clear. Drawing faint pencil lines on the Flipchart will help you keep the writing level.

Tip; Use Blues and Black colours to ensure best visibility. Red and green do show up clearly as well, but be aware that some colour-blind individuals will not be able to distinguish between those colours.

Using flip charts often encourages interaction, especially when the trainer asks for suggestions or contributions from the participants. They work best when there are not too many participants in the class. Remember that they are hard to see from more than about 30 feet (9 meters) away. Flipcharts are essential for group work to report and share their finding to the whole course.

Tip 1: If you pre-prepare a flipchart (with a diagram or slogan) start at the last page and then work forward. This allows you to find what you need quickly and yet conceal it until you need it. You can also use masking tape tabs on the edge of a pre-prepared flipchart page or 'Sticky Notes". This allows you to be able to turn directly to that flip chart page when needed.

Tip 2: By using a pencil to draw the faint lines of a diagram on a blank sheet of Flip Chart paper, your course participants cannot see such marks. This allows you to write in clear lines or a draw a diagram, to a high standard, using a marker pen to trace over the pre-prepared pencil lines you have used.

Tip 3: If you have a diagram on your computer, you can use a digital projector to shine the image on a blank Flip Chart page and then trace the diagram displayed. This makes it easy to produce effective images on a flip chart. Remember, that moving from a screen showing a PowerPoint or Keynote slide to a Flip Chart image breaks the monotony and helps to defeat 'Death by PowerPoint'.

Tip 4: **Use Water Based Marker pens** on Flip Chart pads, as they do not 'bleed' on the next sheet or onto walls when posted with masking tape.

Tip 5: Do not write on the flip chart and talk at the same time. If you do, the flip chart will absorb some of the sound of your voice and you will not see the reaction of your participants to what you are saying. Get into the habit of writing in silence and then turning to your audience to speak.

Whiteboards

Whiteboards can be a real asset to a classroom, if they are of sufficient size and positioned correctly, where everyone can see them. They are excellent for collating suggestions and for displaying Group exercise instructions and Exercise time limits. Everyone can then use the white boards to check the instructions during the exercise.

Tip 1: Make sure when writing on the whiteboard, it is big enough to see from anywhere in the room. I suggest letters should be about 2 inch or 5 centimetres and the writing should be in block letters.

Tip 2: Use Dry-Wipe (non permanent) Marker Pens. If you accidently use a permanent Marker pen on the white board, you might try drawing over the writing with a dry erase **marker!** Wipe off the dry erase **marker** with a cloth or paper towel. It should remove the permanent marker marks.

DVDs and Videos

Using Videos and DVD's can enhance a training session if the subject is appropriate and they are used correctly. Ideal for giving the facts about a case study or exercise when it deals with the subject. Remember you may need to get permission, as many are subject to copyright laws. Using Videos and DVDs add another dimension and again if used correctly will counteract boredom.

Tip 1: Give participants a task when watching the Video or DVD. This ensures that they will pay attention. Example: "I want you to try and identify how many different ways the main character tried to achieve the objective, when watching the next clip". It is important that you then debrief the task at the end of the clip.

You will need to allow time to do this.

Tip 2: Never show more than 12 minutes of the Video or DVD without a break. Shorter clips are even better.

So even if the video is 30 to 40 minutes long, break this down in smaller clips.

Demonstrations

A demonstration is an activity, usually carried out by the Trainer (or an Assistant with the trainer commentating) from which the course participants can observe and learn. When used appropriately it can be very effective. Having participants actually doing an activity helps keep interest and often puts the subject of the session into context.

I have seen and sometimes used demonstrations to train people to

1. Learn how to use a scientific calculator.
2. Learn how to use a computer programme or computer software
3. To read graphs.
4. To conduct interviews and management activities (sometimes called role play)
5. To master physical skills.

When conducting demonstrations, consider the four stages shown below.

1. **Explain**: The Trainer explains the activity clearly. The trainer may use visual aids or handouts.
2. **Demonstrating**: The Trainer then actually undertakes the activity slowly, so the participants can see what needs to be done.

3. **Imitating** – The Trainer undertakes the activity again in a series of stages and the participants follow this by copying each stage.
4. **Practice:** The participants then perform the skill whilst the Trainer observes them and gives advice and guidance

Tip 1: Make sure you have practiced the activity and know the theory behind the activity.

Tip 2: Conduct a risk assessment and be aware of any potential safety implications.

Electronic Aids

I am grateful to Mick Crabtree, M.Sc. for the following description of the Kahoot Program. It is a very useful aid for trainers to check participants' understanding.

Many trainers I know use the Kahoot software and have reported that it is a very popular way of testing what knowledge their Participants have gained. It seems very popular with the Participants too.

TESTING AND REINFORCEMENT

The science teacher noticed that Jones had a faraway glazed look on his face – clearly in another world.

"Jones," he barked.

"Sir?" quavered Jones coming back to the reality of the classroom with a start.

"Are you paying attention?"

"Er… yes sir," answered Jones uncertainly.

"Alright, can you please explain what electricity is then?"

"Um… I'm sorry Sir, I've forgotten."

"What a tragedy," said the teacher, "Jones – the only person in the world who knew what electricity was – and he's forgotten."

Apart from clearly illustrating the disconnect between Jones and his science teacher this hoary old joke also calls into question as to just how the teacher was going to find out if Jones really did know anything about electricity. Had he grasped anything? Had he followed anything?

Classically, Jones would have faced an end-of-term exam where all his shortcomings would be clearly revealed and he would either pass or fail. Maybe, his last minute swatting had paid results and he'd been a lucky in 'spotting' the right questions? But even if he did pass the exam, did he really understand the subject?

But we can't lay all this at the feet of Jones and his science teacher – this is a universal problem. How does a teacher, lecturer, trainer, or facilitator really know if the students sitting in front of him or her have actually understood any of the subject matter?

A key component in any training program is trying to ascertain how much has sunk in – how much have the delegates or students really learned and have they got the right end of the stick. In other words, have they taken on board what you, as the teacher or lecturer or trainer, had actually delivered or have they appropriated something totally different.

One well-tried and proven technique is to make use of what are termed 'Key Learning Points' at the start of each morning, following the previous day's session, in which students, generally in groups, are encouraged to recall a number of significant aspects they had learned from the previous days teaching session. Ideally, these would comprise a number of 'Wow' moments – a "Gee, I didn't know that!" type of illuminative insights from the previous day.

Reviewing or debriefing in this manner is an ideal opportunity to measure the objectives of the lesson or module and ensure that individuals are not stranded at a particular stage in their learning or development cycle. Unfortunately, instead of 'Wow' moments, the list often descends into triteness – a scrabble through the manual or notes to try and pick things they merely remember covering the previous day and not necessarily moments of illumination.

Nonetheless, often what is trotted out, as a Key Learning Point is completely wrong – this is pay-dirt since, in revealing items of complete misunderstanding, any misapprehensions may now be corrected. However, often this correction is a little late in the day since it is relevant to a subject or item that was covered 24 hours or more ago.

Another review system that could be implemented at the end of each module is a series of multiple-choice type questions. This will have a major advantage of immediacy in terms of relevance and allows immediate correction of any misconceptions. This type of debriefing system is almost de rigueur in one-on-one computer-based training because it is so easy to implement. However, in a traditional face-to-face training such tests are really only feasible through the use of handouts and whilst marking the papers is at best only extremely time-consuming, analysing the results becomes a nightmare.

Kahoot!

In recent years a number of solutions have appeared in the form of 'Student Response Systems' that allow students to respond to questions and discussions through the medium of their laptop, tablet, or handheld device – without actually having to raise their hand and speak.

One such a system, an initiative of the Norwegian government, is Kahoot! – an online multiple-choice interactive testing and response system. And, as a bonus, at the moment, in its basic form (which for most applications is all that is required) it's FREE.

Kahoot! may best be described as a non-threatening game-based learning platform. Non-threatening in-as-much that participants remain anonymous making use of nicknames, aliases, pseudonyms or nom-de-plumes such that they cannot be individually identified. Despite this participant anonymity Kahoot! is still competitive and the chance of winning or losing makes it a fun-based experience and keeps students engaged.

Although having a general appeal, Kahoot! is specifically attractive to Millennium/Y-generation students because it's online through their smart phones, tablets or computers. They just have to log into *Kahoot.it* where they are given a game-pin. Once the trainer has the requisite number of logins (displayed live on screen) he/she can then start the quiz.

The trainer sets the time for answering the question – anything from 5 to 120 seconds – which is displayed live on screen.

Instead of answering A, B, C or D there are an array of icons (square, diamond, triangle, and circle) that the delegates need to select on their screens. Once the time period is up the answer is displayed – with the correct one highlighted. The display also shows the number of participants who have selected each answer – with a running total score provided for each participant. Again no identities are revealed.

For the trainer, the resultant display is invaluable since it shows the number of people who got the question right and the number of people who opted for alternative answers. It is now possible to reiterate why the correct answer was, in fact, correct and clear up at any misunderstanding.

The results display clearly presents both the question (shown at the top) and the answers. It also clearly indicates the correct answer with the tick. The bar graph also indicates exactly how many people in the class of 20 obtained the correct answer – imagine it is 16.

However, four people got it wrong. Why? This is where the trainer is now able to dig a little further and ascertain whether this was a misconception, forgetfulness, or merely an erroneous selection. And, more to the point, he can now provide corrective feedback but also reinforcement.

Because Kahoot! is widely used in schools, the creation of such 'nicknames can possibly lead to quite 'immature' responses – with students joining with inappropriate tags. With this in mind Kahoot! maintains a list of words deemed universally inappropriate. Whenever someone joins a Kahoot! session this list is automatically checked to ensure their desired nickname is suitable for use. If it's not, their nickname with automatically be changed to something neutral.

If, despite the automatic filter you see an inappropriate nickname in the game lobby, you can simply click the nickname you want 'kicked' out of the session, and manually remove that player from the game. You may then also use the "Support" link in the top navigation bar to send Kahoot! a message requesting a blacklist of that specific nickname.

Although a student is free to re-join the game lobby after being kicked into the corridor, their personal device now has a red background – allowing the teacher/ trainer to easily identify the offender.

Inputting multiple-choice questions

One of the perceived minor limitations of Kahoot! is that no question can be more than 95 characters long and no answer can be more than the 60 characters long. The aim of this character limit is to avoid excessive verbosity and keep questions and answers short and sweet. This helps to ensure that learners are quizzed on core concepts and are not struggling to understand either the question or the answer.

If, however, this restriction on the character length becomes untenable and you wish to create a longer and more challenging question it is possible to make, for example, a PowerPoint presentation where each slide contains the question you want to ask. Then using your device's screenshot tool you can turn the slides into images and upload them to your questions. However, it should be noted that images do not show until after the answer options have been displayed. Consequently, it may be necessary to extend the question-time limits accordingly.

When actually writing and setting your multiple-choice questions it is, of course, possible to import them directly into Kahoot! However, many trainers already have a complete set of questions and answers contained within, for example a Word document. Alternatively they may prefer to set them out initially in a Word document where they can test them, revise them, and, most importantly, check the character length of the questions and answers. This is performed simply by highlighting the appropriate text, clicking on the 'Review' tag, and then on the 'Word Count' icon. It is now possible to see immediately if the 'Characters (with spaces)' meets the desired criteria of 95 characters (questions) or 60 characters (answers).

Once the multiple-choice questions and answers have been suitably 'massaged' and are now considered fit for purpose they may be cut and pasted directly from the Word document into Kahoot! Be aware that, during this process, sometimes some of the words may be concatenated. This requires you to carefully go through all the material and 'un-concatenate' it.

Sharing Kahoots!

Once you have called up '**My Kahoots**' a list of the sections appears. To the extreme right of each section title is a light blue block entitled '**Share**'.

Click on that and a box appears entitled '**Share quiz with friends & colleagues**'.

Now this is where you need to be careful. Suppose you wish to share with a colleague of yours, Gillian Watts. Firstly, you will need her pass key which **she** would find on the far left hand of the black taskbar on her '**My Kahoots**' page.

Once you are in receipt of her pass key, as you type it in, it's mirrored in a small block below the typing area. When you've finished, you need to click on this mirrored version and only then press **Share**.

IT and network setup

In order to ensure smooth gameplay on secured networks Kahoot! needs access to **ports 80 and 443** on the following domains:

- https://create.kahoot.it
- https://play.kahoot.it
- https://kahoot.it
- https://test.kahoot.it
- https://media.kahoot.it

Kahoot! also requires **secure websockets technology**, which may cause issues with some proxy servers. IT administrators may need to whitelist Kahoot! websockets URLs in your proxy's security settings:

- wss://play.kahoot.it/cometd
- wss://kahoot.it/cometd

SSL is used to encrypt data between devices and servers. Networks that monitor SSL activity sometimes replace our certificates with those of the monitoring service. This can cause authentication errors. The above URLs may need to bypass network monitoring.

Cookies, pixel tags, or similar are used to keep track of progress. These will need to be allowed for our URLs to work properly.

You can test to see if Kahoot! can be played on your network at https://test.kahoot.it/. If Websockets is 'true' and Log is 'Connected', then you should not need to worry about the above requirement.

Setting Multi-Choice Questions

When setting Multi choice questions you should consider the following. Too many trainers fail to consider the following:

1. List only plausible answers, otherwise participants will disregard any such answer.
2. Do not use 'True/False' answers. It is too easy for a participant to make a guess rather than know the answer.
3. Ensure that there is only one correct answer. It is easy to inadvertently include a second correct answer.
4. The questions should test the participant to pick the answer prior to reading the possible responses.
5. **Do not use** a response labelled '**All of the above**'. Participants will be tempted to select this response if they think two or three of the responses seem to be correct.
6. **Do not use** a response labelled '**None of the above**'. This response does not show a participant knows the correct answer.

Tip: It is advisable to get a colleague to check your questions before you use them. It is very rare that you will see your own mistakes. You are more likely to see what you think you have written rather than what you have actually written.

Many trainers I know use the Kahoot software and have reported that it is a very popular way of testing what knowledge their Participants have gained. It seems very popular with the participants too.

There are a number of other electronic programs, such as surveys that trainers may consider using. I suggest you look on the Internet if you have an interest in using some of them.

Having read this section, it will help you to write down at least three things that you found useful and that you might use when training:

1.

2.

3.

Dealing with Difficult Participants & Classroom problems

In reading this chapter, we hope you achieve the following benefits:

You will be able to: -

1. Explain how pre-planning to cope with difficult situations can help to mitigate the effects of such situations.
2. List some of the difficult type of characteristics sometimes displayed on a course.
3. Explain ways of effectively dealing with disruptive behaviour.

The Military and the Police regularly construct negative scenarios in order to be able to train their personnel to cope with such possibilities, should they occur. I am suggesting that trainers should at least think about how they might deal with difficult situations caused by some of their participants during a training session, should such a situation arise. Luckily, nearly all participants are cooperative and most participants wish to learn and benefit from the training session. Dealing with problem participants will occur, from time to time, and by thinking about such situations before they occur, you will be better equipped, mentally to cope with this when it occurs.

Difficult participants are usually unhappy about something and your job as a trainer is to first find out what is causing that situation, if you wish to resolve any problem caused by the individual. The trainer must remain calm and avoid appearing to verbally attack or demean the participant causing the problem. The trainer must make every effort to try and understand the reason why the individual is being difficult and the trainer can only do so by listening to what the individual has to say.

Trainers and their participants develop a relationship over the time that the course is running. Such a relationship is needs driven. It is essential that the trainer develops and maintains a good relationship with all of the participants. If the trainer can detect and observe what the needs of the individual participant is, then the trainer is likely to be able to solve any difficulties that a particular participant brings to the course. To be successful, the trainer needs to observe and communicate effectively with the participants.

Developing learners motivation

Successful learners tend to show a high degree of motivation. Participants that bring problems to a course have a low motivational factor in learning or being there. Participants who feel discouraged often bring their problems into the classroom. When possible, a trainer should try and give encouragement to the participants, this tends to build the participants' self worth. If participants believe that the knowledge they will gain can be applied in a practical way to their work, they will feel a sense of encouragement.   The starting exercise mentioned in chapter 1, may well help trainers see how they can lead participants to see how the knowledge gained on the course will help them in their work.

There are steps that a trainer can take to improve learners' motivation. I believe that the following will greatly assist in achieving this:

1. Showing real respect: This requires the trainer to accept the learners as they are. To demonstrate this, the trainer must not adopt a 'superior' attitude. By the trainer showing the participants that the trainer considers that he/ she is 'equal' to the participants, the trainer will underline a mutual respectful attitude.

2. Open mindedness: If the trainer wants the participants to develop and see the class as being a 'safe learning environment' the trainer must display an open minded attitude.   That is a willingness to see thing from others' point of view. By doing so, the trainer will show empathy and will gain an understanding as to why a participant sees things in the way they do or why they hold a certain attitude.

3. Focus on effort: The trainer must recognise and show appreciation for the efforts made by the participants (not just the outcome). Driving participants too hard will backfire.   Anything that acts

to discourage participants should be avoided, as this will have a detrimental effect on learning.

4. Know the strengths of your participants: If the trainer takes time to find out the individual experiences and skills of the participants, at the start of the course, this can be used to give individual recognition and show respect to the individual. The introduction exercise in chapter 1 will help a trainer gain this knowledge. By the trainer building on the knowledge and skills brought to the course by the participants, an improved course will result.

5. Helpful correction: When participants do not get something right, how the trainer gives feedback will affect the relationship. It is important, to encourage improvement and acknowledge the effort.

6. By asking questions, the trainer can in these circumstances, lead participants to the correct answer. Questions like: "What else might you consider?" "What would happen if you did ....?"

By concentrating on the 6 points listed above, a trainer is likely to prevent participants becoming difficult. However, trainers will, on occasion, even when carrying out training very professionally, come across difficult participants.

It is important, when dealing with a difficult participant, that the trainer does not alienate the group. This is why the trainer must not be perceived to be 'attacking' or belittling the individual. It is important that the other participants see the trainer as being very reasonable and do not rally to the difficult person's side. By the trainer being seen to be reasonable, it is likely the difficult participant will not attract support and will be left with the feeling that his peers think he is in the wrong.

Tip 1: When dealing with difficult participants **concentrate on their behaviour** and not on their personality. It is easier to alter behaviour rather than change personality.

Tip 2: Do not jump to conclusions. What you appear to see may not be the 'full story'. A side discussion between participants may turn out to be an issue pertaining to the class subject under discussion that those involved intend to bring to the group.

Tip 3: Do not assume 'doodlers' are being inattentive. Many people need to be 'active' when learning and I have often found, when questioning a 'doodler' that he/she is fully conversant with current activity.

Tip 4: If a discussion gets heated, remind everyone the need to show others respect. You may need to call a break to allow things to 'cool down'.

Tip 5: Many of the suggestions above may well help to improve the situation, but please remember that quite often the other participants may decide to deal with the problem for you, if given a little time.

Lets look at the type of problems participants can display.

Argumentative Andy: This can be a difficult participant to handle. He appears to look for opportunity to argue and disagree with you and/or others. Some disagreement can be helpful and should be tolerated, but persistent disagreement will damage the learning environment. Do not get into a debate with Andy. It is vital to show patience; otherwise you will be in danger of losing the respect of the rest of the group. Some ideas to help are:

1. Ask the group "Anyone like to respond to Andy's comment?"
2. Show Andy that you are really listening to him and acknowledge valid points, if he has made some.
3. If he is clearly wrong and nobody has voiced a contrary opinion, you may have to say something like "I think we have discussed this fully. Can we agree to disagree about this? We need to move on now, if you wish see me at the break and we can discuss this further."
4. Give Andy a task to do such as recording the main points of a discussion.
5. If Andy continues to argue, then I suggest you talk with him privately. Find out if the course is meeting his expectation. If he makes it clear that it is not or he just does not want to be there, you may need to suggest he leaves the class. If you do so it is vital you let his sponsor and your manager know why you have taken this action, as soon as possible.

Background Bill. This kind of participant hates the lime-light and tries to stay inconspicuous. Shy, withdrawn, quiet much of the time, he is easily overlooked. He will disappear into the background quite successfully. This type of participant rarely causes problems, so why worry about them? I believe we have a duty to give everyone the best training that we can and in order to help Bill grow we need to find ways of getting him to actively participate a bit more. Some ideas to help are:

1. Participation in small groups is much easier and comfortable for a shy person. Getting the class to undertake a small group activity should help.
2. Set up pairs to tackle a learning activity. Ask them to report back in a way that requires each member to give part of the report. This way Bill will interact with his colleague.
3. Occasional ask Bill a question "Bill what do you think about what Mary said?" "Bill I believe you have some experience of this, what is your view?'
4. Make a point of talking with Bill during one of the breaks. This tends to boost a participant's confidence
5. The same question to the other participants in sequence including 'Bill' would avoid putting him on the spot and would give him adequate time to assemble his ideas.
6. Praise for 'Bill's' contribution will positively encourage his future responses.

Complaining Carole: Carole appears to need to complain, blame or find fault with everything. Her constant negativity will have an adverse effect on the atmosphere in the class. She will take very opportunity to voice her negative views. Carole is not a problem solver but a problem finder. Some ideas to help are:

1. When Carole makes a complaint, ask the rest of the class if they agree? If they do not agree, offer to discuss the issue with Carole during the next break.
2. If others agree, with Carole, ask the class to suggest some ways to improve the situation, and then try to incorporate any suggestion for the rest of the course.
3. If Carole makes a negative remark about a person, situation or suggestion, ask her how she would improve the circumstances. If she cannot think of anything, ask the group if they have any suggestions. This will show the group that you are being reasonable.
4. When Carole complains about someone or something, ask her if she knows of any positive points about the person or thing she of which is complaining. Then ask the group to list positive aspects of the situation too. It will often improve how Carole feels

Extravert Eddie: This individual has an opinion on everything and like to share it as soon as possible. The trainer cannot afford to put this individual down. The Trainer wants his enthusiasm to be reined in slightly. Some ideas to help are:

1. Show Eddie that you value his input.
2. Say 'Eddie you made some excellent points. Can we have another opinion on this, before we hear

from you?" Or "We need to get everyone's point of view, can you hold your point for now please?"

3. Show the group that you are treating Eddie fairly and if the group perceives this they may well suggest that Eddie allows others to speak first.

4. Avoid making eye contact with Eddie for a while. This will allow you to pick someone to answer the question or comment first.

Disinterested Derek: Derek seems to be doing other work, reading a newspaper or reading emails during the training session. He is not being disruptive. He may be in the wrong course where the knowledge level is either too low or too high for him. Some ideas to help are:

1. Speak to Derek during the next break and suggest you think the session is not meeting his needs. Find out if there is anything that might trigger his interest linked to the subject under study.

2. Ask Derek the occasional question

3. If he is more experienced, you might ask him to contribute during any questions or discussion.

4. If he is doing other work, he is possibly under work pressure. If this is the case you should acknowledge the pressure he is under and try and get him to appear engaged so as not to adversely affect the other participants.

Dominating Desmond: This participant will 'takeover' if permitted. Politeness and a firm way of dealing with this character will be necessary.

We don't want to shut Desmond out completely. As a class member the other participants could rally to his side if they feel he is being singled out.

Some ideas to help are:

1. The trainer says "Maybe we could get another opinion on this?" This is likely to allow others to contribute.
2. Avoid making eye contact with Desmond for a while. This will allow you to pick someone to answer the question or comment first.
3. Show Desmond that you value his contributions, but you also need to hear other participants' contributions.
4. Show the group that you are treating Desmond fairly and if the group perceives this they may well suggest that Desmond allows others to speak first.

Jeffrey the Jester: Jeffrey loves to be the centre of attention and he tries to achieve this by continually making jokes and funny remarks during the training sessions. Many of his contributions do make others smile, which is, welcome and can help the learning environment. However, he is bordering on being irritating. If left unchecked, the danger is that his behaviour may start to hinder the learning process. Some ideas to help are:

1. Invite Jeffrey to make a comment on some serious course related issue. This will show him that you consider him of value.
2. Praise him when he makes some serious remark.

Kevin- The Know-it-all: Kevin has a need to be heard and acknowledged. He believes he has a lot of experience and wants others to know this. He is not necessarily negative or offensive; his inputs can become a distraction. Some ideas to help are:

1. Allow Kevin to say what he has to say for a few minutes.
2. Ask for other participant's experiences and points of view.
3. Talk to Kevin on a one-to-one basis during a break and let him know that you would like to call on him on occasions. You might also say to him that you need to get quieter members of the group to contribute and ask him to hang back to allow you to get them involved.

Late Louise & Lawrence: A problem that trainers regularly face is that of participants either coming to the course late each morning or returning from breaks late. If you are running a course at a client's premises, then be aware that participants may be told to meet their boss during a break or breaks. I find this a persistent problem. Some ideas to help are:

1. When setting the Course Ground Roles (see chapter 1 'Getting Buy In at the Start") the trainer needs to emphasise the importance of participants returning on time. The Trainer might mention that if participants are persistently late then there may be some late finishing time, in order to catch up.
2. Negotiate a start time. When drawing up the course rules, I ask if the start time is helpful for everyone, sometimes this reveals real difficulties for some participants arriving. Providing **the**

Majority Agree and it does not cause too many problems for others, I have change the start time to accommodate people missing rush hours or coping with child minding issues.

3. Talk to persistently late participants at the start of a break and try and find out why they are late. It may be that they have an urgent family or work related issue to deal with. If so ask them to return quietly and check with you what they may have missed.

4. Thank "back in time' participants

5. Consider using a PowerPoint Timer (can be obtained on the Internet). This software is triggered by the trainer at the start of a break and 'Counts down" the time until the break is over. Many allow you to put various encouraging slogans on them too.

Negative Ned: Negative Ned is superlative at 'squashing' other people's ideas. Anything new or different and he readily retorts, "It'll never work" or "We've tried that before". Often his conversation will start with "Theories like this wouldn't work in the real world". He is negative about everything. Some ideas to help are:

1. If Ned makes a negative remark about a person, situation or suggestion, ask him how he would improve what he is complaining about. If he cannot think of anything, ask the group if they can suggest anything. This will show the group that you are being reasonable.

2. When Ned complains about someone or something, ask him if he knows of any positive

points about the person or thing he is complaining about. Then ask the group to list positive aspects of the situation too. It will often improve how Ned feels .

Non-listening Neil: Neil does not appear to listen to what others have to say. He interrupts everyone and states his point of view very forcefully. His eagerness to participate keeps him from listening. He will have a tendency to interrupt and leap in before others have had their say. He is very eager to give his opinion. He possibly is genuinely interested in the subjects of the course. You do not want to crush his enthusiasm, so you need to deal with this carefully. Neil's behaviour does not help others to learn or to contribute. Some ideas to help are:

1. Make Neil wait by saying: "I would like to hear from Barbara about this please."
2. Talk to Neil on a one-to-one basis during a break and let him know that you appreciate his input. You might also say to him that you need to involve quieter members of the group and ask him to hang back to allow you to get them involved.
3. Ask Neil to comment on what another group member has said.

Rigid Robert: Not offensive in the sense that Robert argues or disagrees but that he can take a stand on an issue and will rarely budge from it. Since he is so unyielding and believes he is in the right the group can find his stance difficult. An idea to help is:

1. It is necessary to get Robert to try and admit there **is** another side to the issue. The trainer might say something like "Robert, as an objective person can you give us any evidence that we can approach this problem in different terms?" Robert is in effect being asked to state an opposing view. This is unlikely to lead to a reduction of his rigid views but will show him that other views do exist.

Side Bar Sydney and Sam: You notice two participants are having a discussion between themselves and it is causing a minor distraction to those participants located nearby. It may well be that they are discussing something to do with the matter in hand, or they could be discussing something outside the parameters of the course. Give then the benefit of the doubt. Some ideas to help are:

1. Remain positive and do not show annoyance.
2. I find that if I stand and remain silent for a few seconds usually works wonders.
3. Move towards their location, whilst continuing to participate in any on going discussion or lecture.
4. Change the activity, maybe by introducing a small group activity where you can put them in different groups.
5. Assume that they are discussing something related to the subject in hand and ask them if they have any question or anything they might like to add.
6. When starting the next session, you might like to revisit the class ground rules.

Tangent Tim: This participant shows enthusiasm and offers inputs that are not directly connected with the matter in hand. The danger is that Tim's input may take participants away from the important issues at hand. Some ideas to help are:

1. Find some commonality with what is being discussed and lead the conversation back to the point at issue.
2. The trainer says"That is an interesting thought, but can we deal with ... (matter being discussed)."
3. The trainer asks others for their thoughts on what Tim said. This will usually show Tim that his thoughts are not 'on topic'.

It is worth having a look at the section on **Psychological Effects of Giving Feedback** in the chapter entitled **'Getting the most from Debriefing'**

Having read this chapter on debriefing, it will help you to write down at least three things that you found useful and that you might use when training:

1.

2.

3.

Dealing with different Cultures

In reading this chapter, we hope you achieve the following benefits:

You will be able to: -

1. Explain how cultures can affect the way participants perceive things differently and how this might affect they way that they learn.
2. Identify potential areas of conflict between participants with different cultural backgrounds.
3. List ways of coping with problems arising from intercultural misunderstandings.

Many training classes are now likely to consist of culturally diverse participants. This is particularly true of courses held in the UK or USA. Many of the courses will attract attendees from across the globe. By effectively managing how different nationalities work together the trainer is likely to actually enhance the learning experience. If a trainer is to successfully gain the most benefit from the participants, then he/she must utilise diversity to enhance learning.

When a trainer becomes aware of the importance of cultural issues in motivating and improving their learners' participation in various learning activities, he/

she will deliver a more comprehensive form of learning to all the attending participants.

Tip: If you know you have participants visiting from other countries, prior to the start of the course, it will pay you to read up on their countries. A good place to start is on the Internet Site: www Foreign travel advice - GOV.UK. If you go to a country listed and then click on "Local laws and customs". Another good free source of information is "The World Factbook" on the CIA webpage, at: www.cia.gov/Library/publications/the-world-factbook/geos. Most countries will have an Internet site that may be worth looking at to gain useful information too.

Regardless of what culture a person comes from, please remember that <u>people are individuals</u> and may not conform to any cultural profile in every respect.

One of the effects of the rise of the Internet, Television and Films is that these forms of media influence most people and this has led to some mixture of cultures. Trainers should recognise the effects of globalisation on the increasing change in cultures and the rate of cultural chance is accelerating all of the time. However, the trainer needs to be aware of cultural differences.

What is culture? I try and keep the definition simple. I believe culture is an integrated arrangement of beliefs, values, norms, and traditions passed on from one genera-tion to the next through learning. *Culture is the means by which human beings interpret their experiences and understand what they see, hear and learn. This is why culture is important to learning delivery, which is so often delivered across cultural boundaries.*

Culture unites people who share a common language, have similar values and often have a common purpose. Due to globalisation, most cultures are in the process of some change.

People with different cultures working together may use different ways of thinking. This has led to misunderstandings, mistrust and frustration. *"For some mysterious reasons, in the face of differences or misunderstandings, we humans tend to read the most negative interpretations into the behaviour of others – they are inefficient, they are not helpful, they are deliberately making us look bad. Mistakes and changing priorities become excuses to 'blame and complain'. When cultural differences are added into the 'human equation', potential for distortion increases. Culture is associated with national differences, but in its broadest sense can be applied to different professional disciplines, status levels, age groups, genders and regions"*[1]. If ignoring the effects of culture is likely to lead to the problems listed above, then I maintain it is essential that everyone connected with learning needs to recognize the potential problems that may arise when training or teaching a course with participants from different cultural backgrounds. The promotion, by the trainer, of interest and respect is essential in any course. To train participants from different parts of the world, trainers cannot apply just their own cultural norms. Failure to take account of other cultures can result in a training disaster.

Tip: If you are a female trainer and have participants from the Middle and Far East, it is helpful if you emphasise your qualifications and experiences in the subject areas being taught, when you introduce yourself at the start of the course. This will help male trainers too, but is essential for female trainers to do so.

Effective communication promotes learning and can lead to tolerance. The Trainer cannot simply group participants with significant cultural differences and then expect them to communicate effectively and without problems. Some participants may well do so, but even more will not. A trainer can help the process by introducing cross-cultural interaction through structured icebreakers (see "Chapter 1 "getting buy-in at the start") and holding a course social event. The use of group exercises early in the course should also help. The more the trainer introduces interaction between the participants throughout the course, the better. Participants exposed to various discussions with people from other cultures, tend to improve their intercultural understanding. With more and more companies trading internationally, this may well be another positive learning outcome of any training event that has a multicultural group of participants.

Communicating is so important, if you wish to establish rapport and understanding. Without effective communication, learning will not occur. Even when we speak apparently the same language, cultural differences can cause problems, so imagine what it is like when the mother tongue of the various members of a course is different. The chances of having 'miscommunication' are enormous. English tends to be the international language of business, commerce and international professional organisations. English speaking trainers need to understand that non- native English speakers will learn a very precise form of English. They rarely understand the slang that native speakers use, or the local idioms.

Tip: When the trainer has non-native speakers in a class, he/she should leave a short pause at the end of each sentence. This allows the participants to mentally translate what the trainer has said.

Tip: If you have Non- English native speaking participants from the same country, it may be useful to consider getting them to sit together. I have found that they often help each other with translation issues.

The trainer needs to use enhanced active listening skills in any interchange that takes place with the participants from a different culture. To be seen to be actively listening helps develop a rapport and show empathy to the speaker. This is vital in developing a beneficial relationship with the speaker.

A reminder of some ways to actively listen is:

11. The trainer suspends judgement about what the participant is saying.
12. Concentrate on the speaker and avoid distractions.
13. The trainer should pause before making a response. This helps the trainer interpret what

is said and allows the trainer to 'fill in' what is not being said.

14. The trainer asks for clarification or for the speaker to elaborate.
15. The trainer tries to understand the feeling of the speaker.
16. The trainer should rephrase what was said, in his/her own words. This is particularly important when the speaker is not a native speaker and may have had difficulty phrasing his contribution.
17. It is important that the trainer listens for the real meaning of what is being said and not just listening to the words.
18. Concentrate on the speaker and what he/she is saying and the trainer should not think about what the trainer is going to say next.
19. The trainer needs to show positive Body Language. That will include:

- Looking at the speaker.
- Displaying an open posture (no folded arms or legs).
- Using Para language (Encouraging noises: 'I see" "Ah ha" "Yes").
- Appearing Relaxed.
- Smiling rather than frowning.
- Maintain eye contact.

Some forms of body language differ in different cultures and this can cause some subtle unconscious irritation by the person perceiving the actions of the person displaying the body language. Hand gestures may have different meaning in different regions or cultures, so be careful in using various finger signals, as they may be very rude in some cultures.

Tip: When dealing with participants from non-western cultures, it is advisable to wait until a woman offers her hand first before shaking it.

Tip: Showing the soles of your shoes, in most Middle Eastern cultures is considered insulting, as is touching peoples' heads. Looking at the Web sites mentioned earlier in this chapter will give you other useful tips on how to deal with people from the countries mentioned.

Tip: Personal space varies drastically in different cultures. Most Western People need a personal space of between 2 and 5 feet (60cm and 150 cm). This personal space increases if they are from remote regions. Middle Easterners tend to have a much-reduced need for personal space. If a Middle Eastern participant comes to talk with the trainer, the natural reaction of a Western trainer is to step back and give themselves more space. This comes across to the participant (often subconsciously) as the trainer 'being 'cold' or finding the participant a 'bit offensive'. If possible, in this situation hold your ground.

Another area of misunderstanding or confusion arises when using acronyms. It is a mistake to assume that even the most widely used acronym in English, will be understood by non-native English speakers. The acronym for that entity may be different in their native language. A golden rule is: The first time you use **any acronym you MUST** explain the acronym in full. Another area that causes lots of communication problems is the use of idioms and slang phrases. I have trained and coached a lot of American and British trainers and too often they tend to use colloquial expressions. I have checked with non-native English speaking participants on their courses and found that on most occasions, they had no idea what the expressions used, meant. It is often assumed that expressions used in films and on television, will be understood internationally. This is a mistake. Expressions, such as "Ball park Figure", "On the Money", "and 'Top whack", are often not understood. So try and avoid slang expressions.

Jokes rarely translate well between cultures. Humour often travels badly, because it often depends on word play and innuendo. This does not often translate well. The British ''banter' often contains irony and/or sarcasm. Many cultures do not understand this form of humour. Some cultures do not use humour during 'serious business' events and view those that do as being flippant. This is not to say that humour is not appreciated by every culture and everyone loves the use of charm.

Time keeping is another area that often causes problems. Some cultures, particularly in Northern Europe and North America, are used to adhering to starting and finishing times. In other cultures, time keeping may be much more fluid. It is important for the trainer to emphasise how important it is for people to start on time, if the learning objectives and course aims are to be met. The trainer may have to accept that some participants will not always be on time. Whilst not ideal, the trainer should not get too upset about this.

Most of the cultural misunderstandings, in my experience, are not between the Iranians, Germans, and Malayan or British participants. The majority of the misunderstanding occurs between people with apparent similar backgrounds, such as the British and the American participants, often with hilarious results. I believe this is because these cultures are similar and each group often make the mistake of assuming their cultures are exactly the same, whereas the other nationalities knew that their cultural norms were different and took time and trouble to check out their understanding.

Tip: Trainers need to be wary of 'apparently similar cultures', because this is where wrong assumptions tend to be made.

Learning traditions also have to be recognised. Many Middle and Far Eastern ways of learning tend to favour the lecturing style of course delivery. Most Western Course participants are becoming more used to the participative style of learning. Trainers may need to encourage a participative style of learning, although many people from these regions may have already experienced this, by attending courses in the West or going to Western Universities. Trainers will need to watch for any signs of discomfort with this form of learning.

I strongly recommend that trainers undertake some research into the history and culture of the participants' countries represented by the course. Know a little about the current affairs and history of a participant's country will help develop the vital relationship between the participant and the trainer. I have seen this on a number of occasions, particularly where the trainer identified a National hero. This made a huge difference.

Tip: If you are visiting another country, then it pays to do a little research about that country. It is advantageous to talk with other trainers who train in that country regularly. They can often help with hints and tips.

Conclusion

Cultural issues associated with learning may seem to be a minefield, just waiting to explode in our face. This is really not the case at all. Increasingly, we are working in multicultural teams, where different ideas, traditions and ways of working add that extra spice and richness to our lives. The corporate demand for training is increasingly global in nature and educators and trainers need to understand the part that culture can add or subtract from the communication process.

Useful books on Culture

The following two books are useful if you want to know more about dealing with people from other cultures.

Barry Tomalin and Mick Nicks, 2007, The World's Business Cultures and how to Unlock them., Thorogood Publishing London ISBN:1854183699

John Mole., 2003,. Mind your Manners, Managing Business Cultures in The New Global Europe, Third Edition, Nicholas Brearley Publishing, London ISBN: 1-85788-314-4

References

[1] Mel Berger and Paul Watts (1994) Management development in Europe, in Managing learning, London, Edited by Christopher Mabey and Paul Iles, P.248, Routledge,

Having read this chapter, it will help you to write down at least three things that you found useful and that you might use when training:

1.

2.

3.

Why bother with Course Evaluation Sheets and how to produce one

In reading this chapter, you will achieve the following benefits:

You will be able to: -

1. List Reasons to employ individual Course evaluation questionnaires.
2. Identifying whether participants believe learning objectives have been met.
3. Explain how to produce a participant Course evaluation sheet.
4. Explain how to use information gained from course evaluation sheets.

Why should you want to have your training sessions evaluated?

I can think of a few reasons why this might be of value to you. They are:

1. To obtain feedback on how you are perceived by the course participants.
2. To gauge whether or not the course material used is of benefit and up-to-date.
3. To gauge whether or not the participants thought the course was of value to them and the job they do.

4. To find out if they would recommend the course to others or not.
5. To find out what improvement in material or teaching techniques might be considered.
6. To permit the participant to see just how much they have learned. (Completing an effective evaluation sheet encourages participants to reflect on what they have gained/ not gained from the course).
7. Using evaluation sheets is a relatively easy and cheap way to gather information.
8. A useful way to see if the facilities used were acceptable.

You should consider how your course maybe evaluated by not just the participants, but also their managers, supervisors and employees. Informal evaluations after the course may have a positive or negative effect on future course enrolments. Your participants who complete the evaluation sheet will be strongly influenced by their feelings and attitudes towards you and the course content. If there is a company course debriefing (and sadly often there is not), the feeling about the course will strongly affect how the client companies see the course being of benefit.

Another form of evaluation that few trainers consider is whether or not the learning objectives have been met. By employing quizzes, key learning point exercises, case study exercises and discussions, trainers should be able to gauge whether or not their participants have achieved the learning objectives. It is vital to have measurable learning objectives for each training session given (see Chapter 3 for more details on objectives).

A much harder form of evaluation for a trainer to gain information (unless you are a 'Company Trainer") is the effect the training has on the work carried out by individual participants, post course. If you have a strong relationship with a company, you may be able to obtain this information; otherwise it is very doubtful that you will. If the effect is noticeably positive, then further enrolments from that company will be forthcoming.

Often participants underestimate just how much they have learned on a course. I have found that the following exercise has a beneficial effect on how evaluation sheets are completed, if run just before you hand out the evaluation form giving the participants time to complete the evaluation process.

Pre-Evaluation Exercise

This exercise, I run as one big group. I ask each person to think about the 5 most important things they have learned on the course. I ask them to write them down in their notebooks or on their computer.

Tip: I remind them that they can use the items they have listed, if a manager or supervisor asks them what they have learned on the course.

I usually **allow about 5 to 10 minute**s for this part of the exercise. I then stand by a Flip Chart stand and ask for a volunteer to give me one of the things he/she has written down. I note this on the flip chart. I then ask for other inputs from different participants. I do not insist that everyone contributes.

I find that most participants want to do so. I then suggest that the participants may want to add items learned to their list of 5 things they originally wrote down. I find that most participants are keen to extend their list of things learned on the course. This enables participants to realise what they have gained from the course, and always has a beneficial effect on their perception about the course. This exercise is another quick way allowing the participants to reinforce some of the learning, all be it, fleetingly.

This whole exercise takes no more than 30 minutes.

What should be on an Evaluation Sheet?

If you are going to have an evaluation sheet what should be on included on it and for what purpose? (Your company or client may insist on your participants completing one they already have).

If you are going to design one then you need to think about the questions you want answered, and how you might benefit from the information revealed. I have some suggestions of things you may wish to think about (and I **have included a sample evaluation sheet later** in this chapter).

How you set up the answers, I believe is important. You need to ensure you do not give the participant the opportunity to select the 'middle of the road' answer. They should be forced to select either a positive or negative response; otherwise many will be tempted to select a non-committal answer.

Areas I think need to be considered are:

1. Pre Course.
2. Learning Environment.
3. Content.
4. Presentation.
5. Relevance.
6. General.

Encouraging participants to complete Evaluation forms

Having an evaluation sheet is one thing; getting participants to complete an evaluation sheet can be problematic. It is important that you try and reduce any embarrassment felt when the participants complete their evaluation form. You should seek honest answers even if they are negative; otherwise it is pointless having the evaluation process and very little will be learned. The form must allow for participants' views to be posted anonymously. To this end, it is useful to have a small box situated in the Classroom but away from where you are seated.

Timing

You should consider timing when you issue the evaluation sheets. If you leave it until the last session of the course (and many trainers do) then participants are very keen to leave and may only give a cursory thought to the questions asked. If the form is issued about one hour before the course is scheduled to finish, you may find you get a much more considered response to the questions asked on the form.

Tip: Do you issue **course completion certificates** at the end of your courses? There are some real advantages in doing so.
   Some I can think of are: -

1. Many participants are required to show their manager/supervisor some documentation that they have successfully completed the course.
2. In some cultures, Course certificates are highly prized.
3. Can be an effective 'bargaining Chip' when getting participants to complete the evaluation sheet. (I usually say "I will exchange a course certificate for a completed evaluation form when I see you post it into the anonymous box")

How do you use the information on the completed Evaluation Sheets?

Once you have received all of the completed evaluation sheets, you should put them away safely. I strongly recommend that you do not look at them until the day after the course has finished. This is because you will be tired after finishing the course and tidying away everything.   When you are tired, even a small criticism may well depress you.

Tip: Often when a trainer runs a course, the trainer will use a lot of adrenaline. I found this is particularly so for me when the course ran very well. I was surprised to find after a very successful workshop I ran in Berlin, that I was very happy just after the finish of the course. The next day I felt somewhat depressed. I mentioned this to a Doctor friend and he explained that he thought I was producing extra adrenaline, during the workshop. The effect of using naturally produced adrenaline was often to result in a 'Downer' when a person stops producing the extra adrenaline. Athletes report similar results after competitions. Having this information helped me cope much better with this problem.

Once you have had a rest and feel refreshed, then examine each evaluation sheet and see if there are any particular trends. Unless there is a major problem identified by the majority of the responses, I suggest that you do not immediately change the course. I have found that participants on one course may make suggestions as to improvement, where as the next several runs of the course, the participants are happy with the content.

Lets look at each section of the valuation sheet shown at the end of this chapter.

1. **Pre Course:** The pre course information needs to be accurate and criticism should be addressed immediately
2. **Learning Environment:** This is a vital area, if you wish your course to go well. These questions indicate whether or not the participants are made to feel at ease, early in the course. Sometimes the room is not ideal (especially if supplied by the client) and you need to make the best of it. If however you are

hiring the room from a third party, then you should have some leverage to get some immediate onsite improvements, long before the participant complete the evaluation sheets.

3. **Content:** The answers to the questions in this area should indicate a course update is due, or that there is an unacceptable gap in what is being taught.

4. **Presentation:** This is an area on which you need to pay attention. If only one or two people show a negative score, then consider it, but do not automatically change anything. If however there are 25% or more answering negatively to one of the questions in this section, then take the matter seriously.

5. **Relevance:** This may indicate that the course is attracting the wrong participants or the promotional material is suggesting the course is at a different level to that which is taught.

Sample Evaluation Sheet (Company Name)

Course Title: _____Location:_____ Date:_/_/_

Name (not obligatory) _____

Please Circle the answer nearest your feelings	Strongly Disagree	Disagree	Agree	Strongly Agree
1. Pre Course				
Promotional material Accurate	1	2	3	4
Course Registration Easy	1	2	3	4
The Course venue information accurate	1	2	3	4
2. Learning Environment				
I was made to feel welcome	1	2	3	4
The Trainer was approachable	1	2	3	4
There were no distractions	1	2	3	4
The Location was neat and tidy	1	2	3	4
I felt happy to ask questions	1	2	3	4
The refreshments provided were acceptable	1	2	3	4
3. Content				
The course materials supported the learning and were up to date	1	2	3	4
The course material was useful	1	2	3	4

4. Presentation

The trainer gave effective presentations	1	2	3	4
The trainer knew the subjects	1	2	3	4
The Learning Objectives were clearly explained & taught	1	2	3	4
The trainer gave effective feedback to participants	1	2	3	4
The trainer promoted involvement & discussion	1	2	3	4
The trainer answered questions effectively.	1	2	3	4
The quality of training was effective	1	2	3	4

5. Relevance

The course has practical value for my work	1	2	3	4
I would recommend this course	1	2	3	4

(Shown in Appendix A if you wish to copy it)

Copyright Gerard A. Prendergast 2018

Having read this chapter, it will help you to write down at least three things that you found useful and that you might use when training:

1.

2.

3.

Evaluating your own performance.

Whilst reading this chapter, you should achieve the following benefits

You will be able to: -

1. Explain the importance of trainer self-development in order to continue to deliver effective training.
2. Explain the importance of continual self-evaluation in order to maintain peak performance.
3. List the most important areas of your training skills that need attention.
4. Produce a S.M.A.R.T. Action Plan to ensure improvements take place.
5. List the advantages of Peer assessment.

Very few people manage to maintain their skill level at a constant. Their skills usually either improve or diminish. By regularly mentally reviewing your training ability and performance, you are likely to make the necessary adjustments in order to keep your skills improving and prevent any decline. By regularly reviewing your strengths and weaknesses in relation to courses you have given, you can decide on what needs to be done to improve your skills and development. If you wish to have continuous improvement then you need to continually review and then revise how you do things. This does not need to be a difficult process. It is vital that you try and improve your strengths and diminish any weaknesses that you or others perceive.

In order to do this effectively, it is important that you make notes (either written or mental) about the main issues of the experience you have had. You might fill out the self-assessment sheet shown in this chapter. What I am suggesting is, that you spend a short time at the end of each day of your course reflecting on what happened:

1. Start by considering what went well.
2. What did you do to make it go well?
3. What did not go so well?
4. Why did it not go so well?
5. This is designed to get to increase your self-awareness, which is the first stage in effective self-development.

Psychologically, it is import ant that you start with what you did well. Otherwise it is likely that you will only concentrate on the negative aspects of your performance. This is self-defeating and you must ensure you recognise what you do well and build on those aspects too. It is as hard to get everything totally wrong, as it is to get something totally right.

Using the Trainer Self Assessment form

This questionnaire is designed be used to assess the way you are conducting learning events. Read through the list of items, and identify areas that you are happy with. Identify areas that you feel you need to keep an eye on. Mark those areas, which you feel need more attention now. It is important to identify your strengths, as well as areas where you feel you need to improve. Regular use of this questionnaire will help you develop all-round skills in self-assessment. You will find it more effective, having identified areas which need more attention if you:

(a). Start by trying to tackle areas which are a bit easier to deal with first.

(b). Try to tackle only one or two of these areas at a time.

(c). Occasionally ask a colleague to discuss your answers to the questionnaire to confirm your own views.

Trainer Self Assessment

Date _____

Activity	Satisfied with this	Could be improved	Needs work	Priority 1st, 2nd, 3rd
Introducing myself to individual participants				
Being Welcoming				
Ascertaining what Participants want from the course				
Finding out Individual's learning needs & delivering these				

Developing participants'
willingness to share ideas and
Information
Making time to talk to
individuals
Listening to participants views
Identifying Participants'
feelings
Giving information clearly
Repeating important items
Confronting unrealistic
expectations early
Using group work to
maximise individual
contributions
Using Pauses when asking
questions
Repeating the question asked
Review Visual Aids
Review Course material
Watch for the 'fidget factor'
Learning Objectives achieved
Encouraging feedback from
the participants

Review Progress on priorities by: Date _____

A copy of the Trainer Self Assessment is in Appendix B.
It can be photocopied and used to self assess

This form is useful to allow you to consider what you
are doing and how well you are doing it. When you
have finished evaluating yourself select a **MAXIMUM
of Three areas** that you are going to try and improve on
when giving your next training session.

Keeping your Knowledge and Expertise current!

Trainers are usually employed because they have the knowledge and expertise in one or more fields. They use their knowledge and experience to be able to develop the knowledge and skills of others.

The human race has progressed technically faster in the last 20 years, than since the dawn of time and that progression is continuing to accelerate. Therefore it is very likely that things in your own field will also continue to develop and change. If you wish to continue to offer up-to-date knowledge, **it is essential that you continue to actively update your own professional knowledge and expertise**. Failure to do so will result in you being out of date and this could lead to real embarrassment in the classroom.

Some suggestions as to how to stay abreast of the current thinking in your area of expertise are:

1. Running a training session is one of the best ways to discover that you have a few gaps in your knowledge of your specialised subject.
2. Subscribe to technical journals in your discipline.
3. Join an Internet forum dealing with your discipline.
4. Join a professional association linked to your discipline and take an active part in it.
5. Offer to become an advisor to a college or university that offers courses in your area of expertise.

It may be useful to give a few minutes thought and complete the box below

> Write a list of ways that you use to keep your knowledge updated here
>
> 1.
>
> 2.
>
> 3.
>
> 4.
>
> 5.

Keeping a Learning Diary

Considering keeping a diary to assist you to develop your reflective ability. Keep it simple; make notes on how you dealt with issues. Note what you thought or felt about issues you dealt with and how you reacted to some of the things you experienced during the day.

Where you make such notes, when and how often you record details is something you must decide on. Your learning diary is private, for your own use. You need to be open and honest when recording details, in order to reflect effectively. You may wish to share extracts with a trusted friend or peer. The sharing this information can be very beneficial, but is not essential.

Taking time to write a reflective diary will allow you to examine experiences. It can be valuable later, to be able to look back on past experiences and understand what was gained from them without the distortion of memory.

When completing your learning diary, you will find it useful to concentrate on:

4. **"What occurred?"**

   Describe the incident.
   "What happened?"

   You need to briefly note what you saw as the issues and what problems were identified. List what were your feelings. Feelings and reactions affect your judgement. This stage needs to be properly considered, if the process is going to work effectively.

5. **"So What?"**

   This stage usually starts with questions like:
   "So what was the result of this happening?"
   "What caused this to happen?"
   "Why was this a problem?"
   or

   "What lessons might I learn from this?"

This stage forces you to draw conclusions from the circumstances you have recorded. It helps to link the activity to your experience. The above questions should identify any mistakes made by you or others that contributed to the situation under review. When this stage is conducted effectively, it will help you gain a real understanding.

6. **"What Now?"**

This stage usually starts with questions like:
"How will I use this information to improve how I train?"

"As a result of what I have found out, what will I change when dealing with similar issues in the future?"
or

"Will this cause me to change how I do things in the future."

This stage of the reflective process should get you to consider how you might include the knowledge learned for use in future training sessions. In order to help you monitor your actions you need to develop an action Plan. Your action plan should include the most important learning points you have identified when you reflected on your recent performance.

Action Plans

You now need to take the next step and take some action to improve some of the areas you have identified. To help you achieve improvement, I suggest you develop a **S.M.A.R.T.** Action Plan. This type of action plan will help you to monitor any progress you make, in relation to areas you have identified as needing the most immediate action.

The S.M.A.R.T Action Plan

The develop this type of action plan you need to:

- Be S*pecific* about what you need to do, i.e. "*Learn and use all of the participants' names on the first day of the course*".
- I must be able to Measure any progress I make "*Did I use all of the Participant's name on the first day*"?
- Can I Achieve this or is it appropriate? "*If I use the breaks and the introductory session, then I should be able to achieve this and it is appropriate because it will show the participants that I value them as individuals.*"
- Is this goal Realistic? "Yes, I should be able to talk with all the participants' on the first day and learn their names too."
- Have I set a Time deadline as to when I want to check on this and achieve it? "*Yes by the end of the first day!*"

Lets now look at each of the areas of a **S.M.A.R.T.** action plan in more detail.

Being Specific

It is very important that time is taken to think about the specific goals you want to achieve. By doing this, you will get a clear picture of what you want to achieve in your training. This will help to keep you motivated and thus help you to achieve the improvements you have identified. A smart goal will help you get into the habit of deciding if what you are willing to work for is something that you really want. Using the Trainer Self-Assessment form will help you to develop goals to help improve the most important areas of your training. By producing goals that are specific, this will help you achieve your plan more easily. Using SMART action plans will encourage you to develop new skills and will likely enable you to seek out new information when attempting to achieve your goals.

Are you Goals Measurable?

How will you know when you have achieved your specific goal? Is it easy to measure? That is why you need to use verbs that can be measured e.g.: Explain, Produce, Undertake, Apply, Organise, and many other verbs that you can actually say "*Yes I can explain!*" or "*I have produced* "to ensure that your goal can be measured.

Is it Attainable?

It is important that your specific goals can be achieved. Will you have time to do the necessary work or make adjustments to achieve them? Do you have, or know where to obtain the information that you need in order to succeed? Can you obtain the goal of your action plan as you desire? To gauge if your goals are attainable when you are producing them, consider whether you have the commitment to achieve these goals?" Are the goal or goals realistic?

Are your goals relevant?

Are your goals likely to make a difference to your training, or are they just cosmetic? With the resources that you have at your disposal, can you realistically hope to achieve what you plan? Do you have to rely on others who may not be available to help?

If your goal is based on someone else's wishes or desires, then it is not going to be one that is going to benefit you realistically in the present.

- Make your goal relevant to what you wish to currently achieve in your life.
- Make sure that your goal is realistic. For instance, if you are not a swimmer and you hate water, then your goal should not be to: "Swim 500 meters in the next two weeks." Set a goal that you have an actual chance of achieving

Set a Time Limit

It is important that you set yourself a timed deadline; otherwise you will find that action gets put off. It helps to have a daily reminder to check progress (computer, tablets and cell phones are useful for reminding us about things we need to look at!)

I find that if I set a two-week time limit, I usually achieve my goals, where as if I make it longer, things fail to get done. If my original gaols take longer, then I try and break that goal into sub-goals and try and achieve each of the sub-goals within the two-week time frame.

Smart Action plans are worth considering. This process can be used to improve various aspects of you teaching and training.

Remember, if you wish to become or remain a top-flight trainer, then you need to continually work at keeping your skills and knowledge fresh and up to date. No one remains at the top of his or her profession without continuing to assess himself or herself and making the effort needed to continually improve.

Having read this chapter, it will help you to write down at least three things that you found useful and that you might use when training:

1.

2.

3.

Concluding your course effectively

This chapter deals with

1. Trainer action required at the conclusion of the course
2. A way to get participants to realise just how much they have learned.

Why is the conclusion of your course important? I think it may have a major impact on how the participants perceive the course they have just completed. This in turn, will influence how they report back to their sponsors, peers and friends. This can have a major effect on your future business, so it is worth taking time to plan how you are going to conclude your course. If you have utilised small group work and exercises during your course effectively, then participants will have exchanged a lot of information with their peers. From a work point of view, these contacts may be very valuable.

Tip: Exchanging Contact details

Organising a contact sheet that the trainer promises to email to the participants is often very much appreciated. **It must be made clear that only people who are happy to share their contact details should complete the form** that the trainer hands around. I strongly advise that the contact sheet contains the following printed message "**By adding my contact details to this form, I agree to this information being shared with other people who have volunteered their personal details.**" I usually have the following heading "Name (Print) Email Address. Agree to share details (Sign)". By doing this the trainer will; comply with various countries' Data protection requirements.

The chapter entitled "**Why bother with Course evaluation Sheets and how to produce one**" has a very good exercise to run prior to getting your participants to complete the evaluation form. In the unlikely event that you do not have an evaluation form, it is worth running that exercise, because it gets participants to realise what they have gained from the course.

Another more visual exercise that a trainer can use, that usually is enjoyed by participants is:

Ask each participant to Draw the following Diagram (I put it on a PowerPoint Slide for them to Copy) Tell them to make it fit a whole page.

Segment circle

In each of the segments of the diagram **put one or two key words:**

1. What I enjoyed most about the course.
2. What I would like to explore further.
3. What was least useful to me?
4. What I learned of most value to me.

I usually allow about 10 minutes for this part of the exercise. The trainer then asks for each person to give his or her answers to segment 1. The trainer may, on occasions, ask each person to elaborate as to why they answered as they did. When segment 1 has been explored, the trainer then questions the participants about their answers to segments 2, 3 and 4. This usually takes about 20 minutes depending on the numbers in the group.

Course completion certificates

It is useful to issue course completion certificates to those participants who attend the course. Many participants are required to show their manager/ supervisor some documentation that they have successfully completed the course.

Tip: Circulate a sheet of paper at least two days before the end of the course, asking participants to write how they would like their names to appear on the certificate. People get very cross if their names are not spelt or shown correctly.

This allows you time to correctly add such names to the course certificates.

Encouraging participants to complete Evaluation forms

Often participants are keen to leave and get home at the end of a course, which is understandable. If you use evaluation sheets you must ask participants to complete them before the end of the course. Your form must allow for participants' views to be posted anonymously. To this end, it is useful to have a small box situated in the Classroom but away from where you are seated.

Tip: Course completion certificates can be an effective 'bargaining Chip' when getting participants to complete the evaluation sheet. (I usually say, "I will exchange a course certificate for a completed evaluation form when I see you post it into the anonymous box") This usually works. If a person decides not to complete an evaluation sheet, then I respect their decision.

Post course Contact

Participants have often asked me for my email address and whether I mind being contacted post course. I have always encouraged participants to do so. I now put my email address on a Flip Chart and say to the Class," *I have enjoyed working with you over the time you spent on the course. You may find that you have further questions about the issues we have considered, when you get home. Please feel free to email me and I will try and answer your queries, provided it is not a major consultation.*" I have found over the years that this offer has not been abused and in fact has resulted in paid consultancy being offered.

Physically saying Goodbye

I believe that the trainer should conclude the course by thanking everyone for attending and for the efforts they made to achieve the learning objectives, whilst on the course. I remind everyone to ensure that they collect all their belongings.

I then position myself by the exit and shake the participants' hands (where appropriate culturally) and wish them a safe journey.

Although you are likely to be tired and probably keen to get on your travels, you should refrain from tidying up, during the final 15 minutes of the course. You need to give your attention to the process of saying goodbye.

Having read this chapter, it will help you to write down at least three things that you found useful and that you might use when training:

1.

2.

3.

Part 2. Blended and e-Learning

This part of the book deals with implementing blended/e-learning in an organisation and why the trainer needs additional training to understand and successfully run these non face-to-face courses.

Considering Implementing Blended or e-Learning

In reading this chapter, we hope you achieve the following benefits:

You will be able to: -

6. List the benefits of blended or e-learning.
7. List conditions needed to ensure effective e-learning Delivery.
8. Explain the difference between tutoring online and in a Face-to-Face environment.
9. List activities that encourage active online participation.
10. List activities that hinder online course completion.

To implement Blended or e-Learning in your organisation

Many organisations are seduced by the major benefits of blended learning and online training. Such benefits are that neither course participants nor tutors need to attend a central location to study or deliver a course and potential to save both time and money by cutting travel time and costs, hotel bills and subsistence costs. Many people fail to recognise that studying in this way is not without time costs, to both the course presenters and the participants. Failures of blended and e-learning wastes time, money and often leads to real learner frustration, with themselves and with their employers. Participants will need to spend additional time undertaking various course commitments and trainers need to actively monitor course participation by their charges.

Many advocates of online training suggest that the online medium is suitable for all kinds of training. Whilst much can be achieved, using various forms of online training, it is important that organisations identify the advantages and limitations of using various forms of this medium. Trying to train subjects that require active dexterity or people reading skills are very difficult to do, using the pure e-learning medium. 'It is useful also to see when a blended learning approach (a mixture of online and face-to-face training) can achieve what a purely online approach will fail to deliver. Using that mixture, whilst it may be necessary, will diminish the savings that a purely distance learning approach achieves. However, for some subjects, it may be the difference between achieving and failing to have the participants gain the necessary knowledge and skills.

Most online courses have a very heavy reliance on content, often very cleverly presented.

The aim of such courses seems to be to transfer data to the participants. To encourage

testing and recall some form of multi-choice questionnaire is offered. Many of these tests are marked electronically, thus further limiting any contact with a tutor.

Very little effort is placed on the learning process. Content high online courses often

suffer from the problem that a large number of the course participants 'switch off'

after a fairly short time. For most human beings, learning is a social activity and the

absence of social discourse seems to lead to de-motivation. As the amount of information people now access regularly, such as the Internet, Blogs, Wickis, Television and Radio, and content high online courses now more than ever bombard an already information saturated population with a further de-motivating process, namely information overload.

What controls whether participants continue to learn on an online course? Often such courses are undertaken in the participants' own time. They start out willing to put in real effort, and sometimes the course content is impor-tant for participants to master in order be able to do their work effectively. This will act as a further stimulus to them completing the course. Even with this initial level of commitment, drop out rates in online learning have been far too high. So what can be done to improve the completion rates? Having run online courses since 1994, Abacus Learning Systems are now getting partici-pant dropout rates of between 3 and 5%. Such low dropout levels are very unusual in any form of distrib-uted learning, and exceptional in the online/ blended learning sector. So why have we been successful? The main reason is because we recognise that learning is a social activity. Our course design ensures that there is contact between trainers and course participants and between participants themselves. It further helps that we have asynchronous (Non-Real time) Chat Rooms to permit everyone to discuss issues, at a time that suits the individuals. This is particularly useful where participants are located in different time zones. In order to ensure that active discussion and sharing ideas takes place, trainers need to monitor and sometimes stimulate discussion. Properly trained blended/e-learning trainers will know how to do this successfully.

When **planning a distance learning strategy**, it is crucial that the decision makers remember that effective training strategy is vital. Too often considerations about information technology have become the dominant factor in many of the strategies adopted by organisations. This has often resulted in a rich information technological environment that fails to capture, motivate or retain the learners. Just because information technology is able to perform certain non-essential training functions is not reason to use such technology. Too often the ability of software to perform administrative tasks has led to it being utilised, even when the training value of such software was dubious. Effective blended learning strategy must give the training needs priority over all other considerations. The ability of any software to perform administrative or other non-educational tasks should be regarded as a secondary consideration.

I believe that the following issues play a major part in determining whether participants find a course interesting, stimulating and worthwhile, or dull, uninspiring and not worth pursuing further: -

Course design,
Pre-course briefing,
Trainer skills,
External support.

When considering employing blended or e-learning, a successful approach is to organise a workshop designed to raise the awareness of the senior management team and the organisation's personnel responsible for staff development. At these workshops, which should include small group work facilitated by the presenter, participants are encouraged to explore the advantages and disadvantages that Blended Collaborative Learning approaches offer, and should explore why this is important. The workshop presenter and, where possible, a staff development officer employed by the organisation, should consider the comments and reactions made by the workshop participants. This approach gives real ownership to the participants and helps to develop a working policy for the organisation.

One of the recurring difficulties is that employers overlook the need to allow participants and trainers additional time to pursue such learning. Managers and supervisors tend not to make time allowance during the working day for such activities, and continue to expect their staff to undertake a full workload at the same time. Such pressures often result in courses not being completed or the individual participant abandoning the course. This

is not the case with face-to-face courses, as the participants are usually away from their workplace and not
usually immediately available to their supervisors. This is
one of the main reasons that blended/e-learning courses
have a poor completion rate.

The drop out rates in many e-learning courses may reach
75%. When participants fail to complete a course, the
organisation squanders time, effort, and money and often
reduces employee 'good will' too, due to frustration and
loss of self-esteem. If you are considering employing either
blended learning or online training, I have listed some
actions that I have found greatly assist the retention of
course participants and thus help to ensure course
completion.

Unless there is serious 'Buy-in' from top management,
any attempt to successfully introduce, blended or
e-learning will fail. When planning to introduce this
type of learning activity into any organisation, senior
management will need to plan to:

1. **Allow participants sufficient time to undertake
   the course requirements, during work time.**

Many organisations have, in recent years, reduced staff
numbers. This has resulted in many professional workers
undertaking a heavier workload than ever before. Such
workers often stay longer at work or take some work
home. On a face-to-face course, participants are taken
out of their working environment and have the time to
devote to the course. With blended or e-learning courses,

employers often over look this fact. This then results in staff having to participate on such courses in addition to their normal workload. With most participants having family commitments to deal with, it is no wonder that such learning is often given a very low priority. Where employers have ensured that sufficient work time is allocated to participants, after negotiating with the course provided, the completion rates are greatly enhanced.

Effective well-trained e-learning instructors/trainers will be skilled at using interactions with individual learners to help them keep their e-learning at a high enough priority to ensure both engagement and success. Interaction between trainers and participants, and between participants, is essential to maintain interest and motivation. For most people, learning is a social activity and most people learn better when they learn with others. This allows learners to share their existing experiences of the issues being discussed and to test out their understanding of new concepts. By participants sharing experiences and understanding of the concepts being discussed they have the opportunity to explain how they might apply new learning to their work. These interactions allow participants to gain different views on what the learning means, often in a practical context. By using e-learning systems that allows asynchronous (non real-time) interaction, this increases the ability for participants to take part in such discussions and gives them time to digest and process the information. This also allows time to consider what other participants are saying about the issue. This is a real advantage over face-to-face or real time discussions, where there is usually little time to think, before moving on to new issues.

Such interaction is vital in any form of distributive learning, as the trainer usually does not have any visual clues as to whether course participants understand what is being offered online. The trainer can only judge understanding by examining the inputs from a participant and by monitoring individual assignments and/or test results. By monitoring interactions from participants, trainers gain an insight into the level of understanding achieved by the individual. It is therefore vital that individuals make regular contributions during the course. Learning tasks that generated discussion usually result in the individual, through the group, achieving a higher level of understanding, arriving at a more considered solution and being exposed to a wider perspective, on the issues under consideration. Just posting large amounts of information on line, like a one way face-to-face lecture, will quickly demotivate participants. The late Robin Mason (1998) believed that "*Others characterise the change required as a move away from content to process: ability to communicate, especially across cultures, ability to work in, form and lead teams, and particularly the ability to find, synthesise, and manipulate information.*" [1].

Potential course participants need to be briefed and if possible be given 'taster' sessions. This will show them how effective this form of learning can be. Without any kind of pre-course exposure to this medium, they may feel that they are being given an inferior form of learning. The provision of technical help and helpdesk support (including learning support) needs to be in place in order to further support learners. Over 90% of my online participants found blended collaborative learning a more rewarding experience than any form of traditional face-to-face delivery. Many said they had more time to think about the issues being discussed, than they would have in a face-to-face course.

If the learning experience is an enjoyable one, course participants are more likely to pursue their learning objectives with enthusiasm and then go on to finish the course. Group learning seems to develop easier in the online asynchronous environment, where people have time to think and develop their ideas, regardless of their personalities or learning style. The more introverted individuals seem to find this medium very user friendly and thus contribute more then they would in a face-to-face course.

The asynchronous type of system allows people in different time zones to learn and interact in groups effectively without one member having to join his/her colleagues at some unreasonable hour. When this type of group learning activity is linked with other forms of learning, such as face-to-face, traditional Computer Based Training (often delivered on CD-ROM) or various distance learning packages, it tends to export the collaborative group learning process to these forms of learning. This blended learning approach uses the online trainer as a conductor of the learning tools orchestra. This permits the most effective learning tool to be used to enhance understanding and achieve the learning objective that was originally intended by course designers. This is because collaborative learning permits and encourages the sharing and accumulation of intellectual knowledge. Through group interaction and debate new ideas, suggestions and solutions are generated. This usually results in the individual, through the group, achieving a higher level of understanding, arriving at a more considered solution and being exposed to a wider perspective on the issues under consideration. It is also more likely to get the learner to link the learning with practical work related issues.

The acceptance by an individual of the collaborative learning process, I would argue, is one of the first essential steps learners can undertake to enhance their understanding of the need for them to take responsibility for their own learning. One of the reasons for this is that they discover they do not need to be trainer dependent in order to learn effectively. They may still look to a tutor for guidance, stimulation and as a valuable resource of knowledge but they will not expect to be given the answers to every question. It has been recognised for some time that **"what I am told, I tend to forget; what I discovery for myself I remember."** Asynchronous group learning reinforces this idea.

Online group collaborative learning allows 'team teaching.' This is becoming more prevalent as many courses now feature multi-disciplinary or multi-faculty inputs. By using blended group collaborative learning, trainers from different organisations and locations can assist the Course staff, without the prohibitive overheads of time, travel and other costs associated with traditional face-to-face courses. Visiting experts can participate for short periods or be available to deal with detailed subject specific issues raised during the course. This is a real advantage

2. **Set very firm instructions to supervisors not to impinge on study time, without exceptional reasons and having disciplinary sanctions where these instructions are ignored.**

Without the active support of the top management team in organisations, blended and e-learning initiatives will fail. Policy makers need to recognise that they will be required to make an investment in time and effort, if this form of learning is to be effective. Without their committed support many of their staff are unlikely to take this change seriously. Such support is essential. Without senior management support, experience has been that more junior managers and supervisors will place a low priority on such initiatives and will often disrupt their subordinates' learning in order to achieve other goals. Short unplanned disruptions can badly affect learning outcomes and course participants' motivation. Asynchronous delivery does allow for some flexibility, but when trying to assimilate new concepts, even short interruptions can have a negative effect on the learning outcome, and often has a devastating effect on the learners' morale. It has to be recognised that there are occasions when operational demand must take priority. These occasions should be relatively rare. In one organization I worked with, when supervisors were suspected of using this excuse to disrupt the time given for learning, the CEO issued instructions that any such disruption would require the decision maker to report the reasons for taking the learners away from their blended course during work, directly to him. This resulted in such disruptions being reduced by over 98%. Successful Organisations that have implemented blended and e-learning, have encouraged their Learning specialists to calculate the amount of time needed to successfully complete these courses and then Senior management has mandated that the employees are given that amount of work time to complete their learning tasks.

The motivational effect of this support has resulted in many employees supplementing this time by adding extra periods of their own time to gain maximum learning benefit. Where the course participant feels that his/her organisation is prepared to put time and effort in supporting this type of learning, it is often highly successful. Sloman (2002) reported *"One of the most important findings was the amount of support trainees received from co-workers and managers for participating in e-learning programs was one of the prime indicators regarding their level of involvement in the programs"*. [3] It has been recognised for some time that without real management support, blended and e-learning initiatives are likely to fail. Oye et al (2012) support this when they wrote *"There are two main groups whose cooperation and support are critical for the development and implementation of e-learning: the management and the learners themselves. Taking time to work with the learners to get their support and ownership will ensure success when the course is launched."* [4]

3. **Give Course participants access to computers and the Internet away from their offices, but close enough to be able to visit regularly.**

The reality often is that a course participant who is trying to study at his/her place of work accesses a course using a computer in their office or work place. They will be subjected to many interruptions, such as a manager or fellow worker approaching them to ask a question or starting a discussion. This then distracts the learner, who is immediately drawn away from thinking about the course concepts. By the time the discussion has been concluded, the learner will often have to retrace his/her mental steps to re engage in the learning. Another serious distraction is the telephone. Whilst it is possible to ignore incoming calls, this requires a lot of self-discipline. Dealing with a single interruption, may not cause too much disruption, but often there will be multiple interruptions, which will result in a diminishing of motivation to continue studying. In one organisation, where I was delivering a course training trainers to be online tutors, despite the participants displaying large notices on their office doors stating **"Please do not disturb – Learning in Progress"** (and various other more impolite requests) mangers and co-workers continued to disturb the course participants, to the point where they were becoming stressed. After a meeting with senior managers, I suggested moving one computer and printer to a vacant office within the building. This solved the problem, as the course participants went to this location when they wanted to access this course. This resulted in their managers and co-workers often leaving notes on their desks, which they responded to at a more acceptable time. Telephone calls went to voice mail and were answered, in due course. Ettinger et al (2006) alluded to this when they stated "*In many companies the demanding work environment makes it harder for training to take place and whilst this affects all training, e-learning is more vulnerable as it relies so heavily on individual motivation*" [5] In another company, the manager put a computer in the coffee room and this work fairly well.

4. **Ensure that all course participants are aware of the costs of these courses and the value that their company puts on such training.**

All course participants should be made aware of the cost to the organisation of their individual training provision. By doing so, companies can help to motivate employees to put more effort into their learning. Employers will often make their learners feel valued and make them feel that the organization is investing in the learner's future. The cost should include 'loss of working time' as well as the costs associated with course delivery. To provide this information requires very little effort and usually has a very positive effect. This can be effective for face-to-face courses as well as blended courses.

5. Ensure course participants are told that they will be expected to submit and 'End of Course' report.

Learners should be required to complete a post course report to be submitted to their managers (and possibly to the people responsible for staff development if different). This report should include:

1. Whether the course was worthwhile or not?
2. Any outstanding issues relating to clarity on any learning point.
3. A list of 'key learning points' that the individual felt he/she gained from the course. (This may very well surprise the individual's manager).
4. And finally, a **S.M.A.R.T.** Action plan (**S.M.A.R.T** stands for specific, measurable, attainable, relevant, and time-based). To cover what the Learner intends to do to incorporate what they have learned, into their work.

Again this should also be required from course participants attending face-to-face courses.

This exercise has an addition benefit, in that it gets the learner to reflect on what he / she has learned. By mentally revisiting the content of the course (which the reporting process requires them to do), they will recall much of what they learned and such recall aids memory in a very positive way.

Such reports allow the organisation's course purchasers to gauge whether or not the course offered was worthwhile and value for money.

6. Actively develop support from the organisation's I.T. Department.

Too many organisations fail to realise that implementing blended/e-learning learning will have an impact on the work of their I.T. Department. The I.T Department' mission is to ensure the computer networks and critical computer applications run continuously, smoothly and securely. They are often burdened with carrying out upgrades of hardware and software. They often have little knowledge or understanding of a trainer's requirements for an application that will deliver interactive blended/e-learning. It is important to remember that the staff of the I.T. Department will 'own' the Servers, Networks and computers used to deliver the system. Although I have found that where companies allow learners to access their e-learning system from home on the learners' own computer, many learners will give more of their own time to studying on such courses.

Tip: If you are likely to run one of the first blended or e-learning courses in any organisation, then I strongly advocate that you make every effort to engage with the I.T. Department staff and try and get their 'buy-in'. They have the ability to help or hinder how well the computer side of the course runs, and I.T. provision is a vital component of any blended or e-learning delivery system.

In order to ensure that the organization is getting a reasonable return on its investment from the training, some form of post course evaluation needs to be carried out. As Davis et al (2008) states *"Ideally, the development of an e-learning system should include a plan for the independent evaluation of all aspects of the system, but especially the degree to which it enables or enhances the achievement of the stated learning outcomes (especially in the opinion of its users). Furthermore, such an evaluation would also provide information about the system's return on investment, especially the unanticipated or unseen costs of implementation from back-end systems, staff attitudes, infrastructure, and so on."* [8] Too often organisations do not carry out post course evaluations and do not know whether the training to purchase or provide delivers a worthwhile result!

Having read this section, it will help you to write down at least three things that you found useful and that you might use when training:

1.

2.

3.

Training the Trainer to deliver Blended or Online courses

When the movie camera was invented, the early filmmakers used the new cameras to film plays. They employed their existing skills and knowledge in the only way they knew how at that time. Through years of trials and experimentation they evolved more ways of exploiting the medium. The movie camera now permits a great many additional techniques to be exploited in order to enhance the audiences' experience. Over time, a whole new way of operating has been developed, in order to exploit the film medium fully. How a film is made today is significantly different from the way that a play is produced. Some of the core features in the production of plays and films remain the same. The course training skills between face-to-face and blended/e learning are the same, but there are subtle differences, particularly where a trainer wants to fully exploit the e-learning/distance learning component of blended/online learning. With the medium of online group collaborative learning we have developed training techniques that will reap the learning benefits that the online medium may offer. By linking e-learning with other forms of learning delivery we can achieve Blended Collaborative Learning.

The idea of participants learning in **collaborative groups** is not a new concept. A number of organisations have explored the advantages gained by using a form of virtual groups. In the academic world the approach is known as Computer Supported Collaborative Learning (CSCL), in conjunction with computer based message conferencing, which is known as Computer Mediated Communication (CMC). My preference is to simplify the description and talk about 'Group collaborative learning'. The approach has become the foundation on which successful Blended Learning programs are constructed. Group blended collaborative learning actively encourages the modern form of 'communities of practice 'and permits dispersed individuals to contribute and gain from this kind of group involvement. This is similar to using small group work in face-to-face courses. By embedding human interaction in learning programs, the online trainer exploits the human need for socialisation to aid learning.

Group collaborative learning delivers positive interaction when there is active and persistent tutor facilitation taking place on asynchronous computer conferencing systems that operates small groups. Grundry (1992) defined collaborative learning as "…. *individual learning as a result of group process". At its heart it is the process by which people learn as a result of interactions with their peers. It is important to recognize the contrast between the collaborative learning model and the transmissive model of traditional formal education, in which interactions occur principally between the teacher and participants. In the strict transmissive model, peer-to-peer interactions are not seen as relevant to learning, and may even be discouraged.*" [6] The use of asynchronous computer chat rooms facilitates and encourages dialogue, even by course participants with more introverted types of personalities, provided the subgroups are structured in certain ways. The subgroups I am referring to are constructed from the course participants and must be small enough to ensure active participation by all the subgroup members.

Tip: Online groups should be made up of between 4 and 6 participants where possible. Bigger groups, we have found, encourage one or two people to dominate, where small groups of two and three can be effective. Having at least 4 participants tends to ensure the groups' actually construct further knowledge and thus increase learning. By organising the participants into small subgroups, effective group dynamics create a climate for successful collaboration. Where there are more than 6 participants in a group, this seems to encourage some participants to "lurk"; that is to read contribution but then fail to contribute or comment. This makes it impossible for the trainer to be able to assess what the 'Lurkers' understand about the issues being studied, without some form of further test. It has also been found that non-contributing participants also tend to be more likely to drop out of the course. Another reason to keep the group below 7 members is that of information overload. The problem of information overload, which often bedevils online learning, is also minimised. Larger groups create too many contributions for most people to read properly or a small number of participants end up dominating the discussion.

Having the ability to utilise online group collaborative learning means that the organization can deliver learning in a number of ways, blending various mediums. The organization can use any form of learning delivery that is appropriate and available e.g. blending face-to-face experiences with synchronous online tools, asynchronous online methods and even Computer Based Training knowledge objects in an appropriate mix. The tutor becomes the conductor of an orchestra of learning tools and may use the appropriate tool to try and achieve maximum learning, at any point in the programme when such learning is required.

By harnessing the benefits of asynchronous computer chat rooms, learner access and flexibility are maximised. Using this non-real time approach, experienced online trainers, using effective course designs, will more easily cater for the various learning styles of participants. Trainers do this by designing various exercises that cater for the needs of the different learning styles. This will occur if, and when they learn to mix the different types of exercises in an appropriate way.

Too many early online learning approaches placed technology at the center and relegated the function of the trainer to a subservient role. As Milner and Draffan (2000) of the British University of Industry point out "*University postgraduate departments have realised the benefits of having tutor roles that check up on the progress of all work-based learners. Of course all of this helps retention but we all know that this human encouragement is essential for effective learning.*" [7] I would argue that the need for this trainer role is vital whenever a learning need is to be satisfied by a structured experience. This applies as much in the corporate training sphere as it does in the academic arena. Active online trainer activity will stimulate interest, discussion and learning.

Blended Group Learning can be defined as a trainer led distance-learning method that blends available face-to-face and online techniques on a foundation framework of facilitated asynchronous conferencing. It delivers learning goals efficiently and effectively and is capable of helping learners construct knowledge.

A skilled e learning trainer is required to ensure a successful outcome.

The trainer is the trigger to foster or stimulate online learning, not the technology. If used appropriately, technology is just a tool that permits facilitating trainers to encourage learning in a flexible and imaginative way. The help and encouragement given by peer support that online trainers should encourage will often determine whether learners complete their courses successfully. The online group learning process combats the 'loneliness of the distance learner' and helps to ensure that the number of participants completing the programme remains very high. Blended group learning helps to ensure that social activity is fostered and encouraged as a main part of the learning process. It also has another very important benefit, which is explained by Mallinen (2001) "Social *interaction skills are increasingly important in a modern world. There is also evidence that learning is improved by interaction with other participants. This seems to be one of the most important ways that IT can enhance learning.*" [8] Knowing that social interaction is so important, very little effort has been committed to enhance the skills of trainers in this vital element in online learning. There is still too little recognition that online course deliverers need additional skills and knowledge when delivering any form of online learning or blended collaborative learning. Most trainers have never had the opportunity to study using a form of e-learning, unlike when they deliver face-to-face courses. Face-to face trainers will have spent many years studying traditional courses and subconsciously will have learned lessons as to what works and what does not from a training perspective.

When reviewing efforts of blended or online courses offered at various universities, government departments and business organisations, I constantly see large dropout rates, where untrained deliverers have tried to use the 'content high' model to deliver learning online. The 'content high' approach to online learning is where material is placed on a web page and the success of learning is, in the main, often checked by the use of computer marked multi-choice questionnaires. With this approach, there is little interaction between course participants. This approach is becoming increasingly discredited. This is because participant non-completion rates on such courses are unacceptable. Every unsuccessful course participant is likely to further damage your organisation's effectiveness. and the reputation of e learning as a whole.

Preparing trainers ready for Blended or Online training

Most people are very uncomfortable when asked to cope with changes in the way they work, particularly when they have mastered the skills needed to teach effectively in a face-to-face environment. When there appears to be very little support to enable them to cope with the imposed change, and no certainty that the proposed methods will ultimately prove successful, they are likely to put minimum effort into acquiring any additional skills needed. Much of the change in Corporate Training is seen as externally driven, for non-pedagogical reasons. Mason (1998) echoes these thoughts by writing that "*Others characterise the change required as a move away from content to process: ability to communicate, especially across cultures, ability to work in, form and lead teams, and particularly the ability to find, synthesise, and manipulate information.*" [9]. A big mistake often made is that the trainer, who will actually design and teach in online learning programmes, is left out of formulating the changes. They are not consulted and the change appears in the form of a 'dictate'. Most people seem to find it hard to 'buy-in' to anything in which they believe they have little or no say in what is being changed. Intelligent people have the ability to subvert, or at least fail to put effort into anything in which they have no ownership or belief. Without the active 'buy-in' of the trainers tasked with delivery of the new blended or e-learning course, failure will occur.

The introduction of blended or online learning requires, if it is to be effective, considerable time and effort to be spent on preparing trainers to cope with the new ways that they will be expected to operate. Most organisations will be forced to implement some form of learning that has flexible element. Such training will probably encompass a major element of online learning, to cope with the increasing training demand, to maintain a skilled workforce. Many organisations have tried to produce effective online learning by converting lecture notes, or other paper-based materials, to material that can be placed on Web pages, accessed via the Internet. This approach is what I call the 'content high' approach. Eisenstadt and Vincent (1998) seem to concur, "*Simply translating material from familiar media into electronic form is rarely productive – and is certainly inadequate for supported distance education, which aims to engage the participant in a 'community of learning'. If we hope to improve, rather than translate, we must understand the whole teaching and support process through a critical examination of its functions*". [10]. Simply reading material online and then completing a multi-choice questionnaire, will not prevent participants from failing to remember, learn or complete the course.

Few instructors and trainers will embrace anything that they consider to be untried and of doubtful benefit. In my experience, a more successful approach that works is to hold workshops designed to raise the awareness of corporate trainers. At this workshop, which must include small group work facilitated by the presenter, instructors and trainers are encouraged to explore the advantages and the disadvantages that blended group and online learning has to offer. The workshop presenter and, where possible, a training manager employed by the organisation, should consider the comments and reactions made by the workshop participants. By employing small group work in the workshop, this permits the workshop presenter to: -

(i) Correct any misunderstandings about the advantages and disadvantages that the workshop participants may have gained from the presentational part of the workshop.

(ii) Permit workshop participants to start to see where this form of learning delivery might be employed in their particular areas of responsibilities.

(iii) Get participants to start to consider what skills they already possess that could be utilised to implement blended group or online learning and what extra skills they might need to acquire.

With the help of the organisation's Training Manager, who would be a valuable observer, the presenter should be in a position at the end of a workshop to decide which: -

(a) Trainers are enthusiastic about the prospects of employing blended group or online learning techniques.

(b) Trainers whilst not being enthusiastic, are open minded about the possibilities of using Blended Collaborative Learning techniques.

(c) Trainers do not appear to believe that Blended Collaborative Learning is necessary, workable, or desirable.

These observations are extremely useful, because they permit the organisation to concentrate the training and efforts, in the first instance, on trainers who fall into the (a) category above. Enthusiastic staff will volunteer to undertake the necessary additional training without making demands that may cause difficulties. They are also much more likely to devote the time and effort to successfully complete the necessary additional training. By introducing blended group or online learning with enthusiastic trained staff engaged in the delivery, organizations are more likely to produce and deliver successful early courses. They will have a number of 'champions' who willingly promote the advantages of this type of course delivery.

If the first courses delivered by a Blended Collaborative Learning approach are unsuccessful, this is likely to stop, or seriously hold back, successful implementation. Failure strengthens the belief of people who fall into the (c) category above and is also likely to adversely affect the opinions of everyone in the organisation. Successful early courses have the opposite effect, especially when the first group of learners promotes their success amongst their colleagues, which they have a tendency to do. When this approach was adopted, it led to the enthusiastic staff members (category a) willingly pioneering and then promoting the blended learning approach. This then led to a growing number of open-minded people (category b) becoming more enthusiastic about this way of course delivery. Over time this has led to many of the skeptical staff members (category c) revising their views and even seeking to be trained in the techniques needed to deliver this form of learning approach. Nothing succeeds like success!

Such a workshop also permits the organisation to discuss what arrangements it needs to make, to accommodate the extra additional work load that is required to provide this form of course delivery. It appears to be more effective to have an external presenter to run this type of workshop. Having run many such workshops at various universities, government agencies and corporate organisations, I am continually surprised that what I have to say appears to be accepted far more readily than when similar workshops are run by internal staff members. There may be an element of "a prophet is never recognized in his own land" about this. The other element is that workshop participants are likely to ask questions that will establish very quickly if the presenter has a thorough experience of delivering successful types of courses. People with no actual experience of delivering online learning are often quickly discounted, especially by practicing trainers. Having an external facilitator at an introductory workshop appears to empower the participants to be more questioning about the advantages and disadvantages of blended or e-learning. This then gives the organisation's leaders a clear view of those trainers who will proactively promote this form of training.

Many organisations **fail to plan for realistic training of trainers** when introducing this medium, because they assume that their instructors and trainers do not need any additional skills to teach online. This often results in people with little, or no, understanding of the medium being expected to undertake tasks for which they have insufficient knowledge. The hardest part of introducing this type of learning is to motivate and train the trainers.

In practice, I believe this is the main reason why so many online initiatives have been very slow to develop, or have been unsuccessful.

Enthusiastic blended/online deliverers are often expected to develop their online skills and design online courses in addition to their already demanding traditional roles. Innovators were rewarded with extra work. This leads to open minded people (category b) declining to become involved. The result is that this method of course delivery is relegated to the margins of the organisation's activity.

In this form of learning, the course deliverer will be much more of a mentor than a teacher, trainer or lecturer. Most experienced blended / online trainers recognise that they need to undertake far more of a 'hands off' facilitator role.

There is the question of added value for the participant when using blended/ online learning. Participants become more actively involved in exploring the various subjects being studied. I believe this is because participants have more time to think before responding. Participants tend to receive more individual attention from the tutor in this form of learning, when conducted effectively.

Another advantage to a trainer, who is skilled at running courses using blended/online learning, is that the trainer may take part in the delivery of courses, in collaboration with institutions/ organisations in other parts of the world, without having to spend time and money on travel. It may also provide sufficient partici-pant numbers that is needed to develop and run a cost effective course.

The ability of an organisation to run an effective course worldwide is already a reality. This means that traditional 'catchment' areas are no longer a significant factor in the recruitment of participants.

Getting Started

How many people undertaking mountaineering for the first time, would attempt to climb Everest on the first day? Yet many trainers acquire some conferencing software and then try and design and run some kind of pilot 'online' course, without ever having experienced any form of online learning, even as a participant! When participant drop out rates climb, or the final results are less than impressive, trainers and often training managers who encouraged them, without supplying any form of training or practical support, rarely recognise the lack of professional development as a key element. They start to believe that the medium is not very suitable for learning primarily because they do not have any experience of studying using this form of learning. This contrasts sharply with their face-to-face learning experiences, which they subliminally draw upon when conducting a traditional class. A very common mistake that many trainers make is to assume that what works well in their face-to-face sessions can be transferred easily to some form of online learning delivery system. I believe it is essential that trainers have an opportunity to experience collaborative learning online, as participants. This will get them to sample some of the differences first hand. Undertaking a course of study needs to be of sufficient length if it is to be beneficial. Courses that train trainers deal in blended and online learning issues over a

10 weeks period, are likely to give them a real insight and 'feel' for this medium. Such courses have been available since 1995 and have been delivered to universities, government departments, corporate training departments and independent trainers. This type of course should permit participants to experience the advantages and disadvantages that their online participants are likely to face. Being exposed as online participants makes trainers more sympathetic and supportive when they eventually train online, themselves.

It is helpful if the course starts with a one-day face-to-face workshop, as this is the form of learning that they are familiar with. The day is structured with the intention of exploring, sharing and reducing the trainers' fears. It also permits them to be able to learn how to use the basic functions of the conferencing software with readily available 'hands on' assistance. Group dynamics often start to develop on the initial face-to-face day. Attendance at this day is not essential, and many courses have had participants from Asia or America who just could not attend.

There appears to be a major psychological difference between IT technologists and trainers. Computer technologists deal with processes that are, in the main, in a linier fashion, such as computer programs. Most trainers are 'people' people and think in patterns or a non-linier way. I believe that this is why there is some dichotomy between trainers and many computer scientists and technicians. These groups may often speak the same language, but the words used appear to have a different meaning, or maybe the groups just interpret what is being discussed in a different way! This has often resulted in most technology delivery platforms being highly developed in a technological sense, but not very intuitive when employed for use by trainers. Many technologists consider learning to be a matter of information transference, rather than a process for gaining deep understanding.

Many systems on offer appear to be Computer Based Training (CBT) delivered on the WEB. This is little different from many of the programs delivered via CD-ROM. They have a place, but they do not exploit the benefits of Information Communication Technology very well. People interacting with people make the major difference to learning, whether this is face-to-face, or, online. Members of institutions and I.T. departments should not be neglected. Efforts need be made to get them to understand the importance of group discussion, peer collaboration and the ability for trainers to be able to interact in a facilitative way. Too often, implementation plans fail to consider the importance of giving their I.T. personnel a chance to share their views and the needs of the faculty members. Unless included in the initial discussions, IT staff may well view the introduction of yet another software system, as onerous and time consuming on an already stretched IT staff department.

When implementing blended/ online learning, is essential to try and reduce the fear many trainers have of computer technology. This has become far less of an issue in the last few years, as most trainers have embraced computer technology, in it's various forms. If technology is introduced as a tool that permits trainers to reach their participants in an interesting way, this can help. The person who trains the trainers selected to deliver this form of training needs to be someone who has a deep understanding of the problems and concerns of trainers, particularly in relation to the introduction of online learning. It is important to encourage training staff to build upon their existing strengths. By demonstrating how to use the electronic tool to build upon training staff's existing skills, one is more likely to diminish many of the understandable fears that some have. Diminishing fear is essential if trainers are to make a start at developing the necessary knowledge and skills to effectively deliver blended/online learning. Many trainers will give a number of reasons as to why they think that online learning is a 'flavour of the month' and not a serious method of learning delivery. This often hides their fear of the technology involved in the medium, sometimes even from themselves.

The aim is to encourage training staff to be able to communicate, study and collaborate with their participants using the technology with the minimum of fuss. I believe that by giving trainee trainers a meaningful group-learning task at an early stage, they will start to experience how they can utilise their time in thinking and formulating their ideas. This task should only require them to be able to log into the conferencing system, read a message, send a message and then log out. This can give the future online trainer an intrinsically rewarding learning experience, without requiring them to make a major commitment to learning complex computer programs. Early success is vital to encourage further learning gains, especially in the use of computer technology.

A participant on a previous course put this very well"
"When I enrolled on to this Course, I felt I had very little experience of computer technology, however I was soon to realise that some of my fellow participants had never switched 'the box' on - my first lesson, if they were willing to try so was I. My first task was to discuss my hopes, fears and expectations of the course, how reassuring to discover others felt the same way.

What really fascinated me was how quickly I became an online 'Junkie' and how my thoughts differed from those of other peoples. By reading fellow participants inputs I soon discovered how my own thoughts could be challenged, how I could enlighten my views and broaden my horizons by 'mulling over' other people's opinions." [11] It is essential that future online trainers get a real feel for how the online medium can affect learners. It is of a further help if they are provided with support and guidance from knowledgeable experienced online trainers. Trainers who have not been trained to use participant centered techniques will have to learn how to facilitate, if they are to become successful at creating and delivering blended/online learning.

Developing the Online skills.

Many effective face-to-face trainers are still not well versed in the use of basic online trainer skills. They need time to develop some very basic skills and more importantly, confidence in their ability to deliver online learning. We encourage participants to adopt the 'little and often' approach. This is to connect to the conferencing system for short periods and as often as possible.

Psychologists consider that most people can assimilate between 5 and 9 new concepts at any one time. Trying to get participants to learn too many software features early in a course will be counter-productive. Trying to introduce too many 'features' tends to confuse people. This leads to frustration and sometimes to a feeling of personal inadequacy, particularly in relation to the use of computer technology! Again, this aspect of e-learning problems has continued to diminish, as more and more people have become active computer users.

It is important at the start of a course, to cater for participants who may have initial teething problems with their computer equipment or their ability to connect to the conferencing system. It is important to provide help, either by a telephone help desk or online, if appropriate. By leaving the more important concepts towards the end of this module, participants with initial technical problems are less likely to miss participating in vital learning stages.

Once all the participants have surmounted any of the initial teething problems that often occur, it is useful to introduce small group collaborative exercises. A typical early exercise might be posted to a course module and written in the following manner: -

TASK X – FIVE CONCEPTS

There is a fair bit of reading to do for this task. It is important to get the reading done early and make notes as you read - if you are going to contribute early and get a discussion going. Everyone should post his or her ideas, including the summariser.

(For each task, one of the group is given the job of summarizing his/her group's discussions and posting this to the main area. This permits the other groups to see what the group has discussed. It also helps motivate each member of the group, because they each know that they will need the help of their peers when it is their turn to undertake the summarizing task. These group summaries may be likened to an electronic flipchart!) Netweaving is the art of being able to link together many points in an online discussion. Some of these will have very tenuous links (typically found in online discussions). Undertaking the summariser's role permits online trainee trainers to gain some practice at employing this art.

"It would help if you post a message to your group on the aspects you found of interest in the course reader (as early as you can).

Using the course reader (Title: XXX), please read the Chapter 1 paying particular attention to the section on CMC in Education and Training, which starts on page 17, and then Chapter 2.

(Note that the course readings are supplied to the participants in hard copy format – as books–. This avoids participants having to print out long texts. It just places an extra burden on them, which is often resented! It also gives them a break from working on the computer, which is important)

Then post to your group

three ideas or concepts from the readings in the course reader that is of most interest to you and give reason for your choice.

Then comment on the contributions of colleagues in your group.

I would ask the summariser *(Group 1- Name and Group 2 -Name and Group 3 - Name), to try and complete this task by midnight on Wednesday 3rd October and post it to the main Module 2 conference area

I hope you find the material of interest. You'll find some relevant material in the online library (via the conferencing software if you still feel like reading more material on these issues). Do not hesitate to ask me for further readings.
Regards

[Tutor's name]"

These exercises permit participants to experience the ability of forming social relationships, using computer chat rooms. They often witness 'real process' taken place in these early online discussions.   There is something about the medium that seems to encourage more open responses. Maybe it is the lack of the embarrassment factor due to the lack of body language?   Participants may start to notice that there is a much more even spread of participant contributions than usually experienced in a conventional class.   This may be because of the 'built-in' time delay, in this form of asynchronous communication; the more extrovert participants are not able to dominate discussions and activities, as they often do in face-to-face training sessions. The more introverted participants (Theorist, or Reflector learning styles, as used in the Honey and Mumford Learning styles theory) tend to contribute much more than they would do normally. Trainee trainers who read about a concept gain something, discussing what one has read with one's peers are a much richer learning experience.

Trainee trainers need to experience the use of small groups to prevent a common problem that bedevils online training – that of Information Overload. As Pincas (1997) states "*In order to allow this kind of fruitful collaboration, it is important for the participant groups to be quite small, otherwise the number of tasks and messages become too difficult to follow. Just as in f2f contexts, a discussion among more than 8 or 10 people is unlikely to succeed if all want to play a role in it.*" [12]

From experiments conducted on group composition over several years, I have concluded that group size is a key factor in creating the collaborative environment; and I now advocate groups of 5 or 6 people. This seems to be supported by work carried out by Professor Simon Garrod of the University of Glasgow who advocates that groups of up to seven should be used for collaborative tasks such as producing innovative creative solutions to business problems. This is reported by Fey et Al (2000) "*Current models draw a broad distinction between communication as dialogue and communication as monologue. The two kinds of models have different implications for who influences whom in a group discussion. If the discussion is like interactive dialogue, group members should be influenced most by those with whom they interact in the discussion; if it is like serial monologue, they should be influenced most by the dominant speaker. The experiments reported here show that in small, 5-person groups, the communication is like dialogue and members are influenced most by those with whom they interact in the discussion. However, in large, 10-person groups, the communication is like monologue and members are influenced most by the dominant speaker. The difference in mode of communication is explained in terms of how speakers in the two sizes of groups design their utterances for different audiences."* [13] Less than 4 people tend to restrict the interchange of ideas. Each course would have many such groups, supervised by the same trainer. I have found that groups with more than 6 members tend to end up having 2 or 3 people who contribute a great deal and others who contribute little or nothing. Using a technique that I developed, I successfully encourage groups of 5 or 6 people all to contribute. This also helps to prevent drop out rates.   If there are more than 6 people in a group, I have found that one person tends to become a 'browser' (someone who reads others' contributions but fails to contribute to the discussion – also known as a 'lurker'). 'Browsers' are much more inclined to 'drop out': I believe that they may feel that they are not part of 'the group' and consequently fail to invest the required energy. I accept that not all 'browsers' drop out. Focusing on continuous collaboration in small groups and discouraging browsing, I have managed to reduce our drop out rates to between 3 and 5%.   With the high completion rates come what appears to be far higher success rates than achieved by other learning methods. I am personally of the opinion that formal evaluation studies are needed and will demonstrate that blended group online learning is a major pedagogical breakthrough.

Contributors often resent browsers, because they are usually seen as 'freeloaders'. Larger groups are more difficult to manage, with many of the others then ceasing to access the group discussion. This is why, by breaking the larger group into small sub-groups, the essential environment for effective collaborative learning is created and managed by the trainer.

Online trainer training should be introduced to give trainers a chance to carry out tasks designed to enhance their skills in communicating with groups, using computer conferencing software.

Another advantage is that this type of online trainer training permits trainers to experiment with their own online style of delivery. It gives them the chance to identify differing personal styles and assess how their peer group may perceive a particular style. It is important that future online trainers get sufficient exposure, as online participants, to give them first hand knowledge of many of the advantages and disadvantages of this medium as a learning tool. Such training should also expose the trainee trainers to the various techniques that assist in creating a learning community that motivates peer collaboration. This would include how to creating a friendly, social environment, and the importance of acknowledging the early participant contributions. Another important stimulus is giving supportive feedback and fostering the various discussions in small groups, by asking appropriate questions.

An important additional trainer input is the concept of the individual course participant online tutorial. This is where the trainer can review and give supportive critical feedback on the efforts made by the individual participants. This can result in the development of the individual participants online portfolios. Trainee trainers should experience the different types of reflective individual online tutorials during their training. This gives them personal experience of this very powerful reflective learning tool. The disadvantage of using this technique is that it does take trainer time to undertake effectively.

Most trainers deliver some very successful traditional learning experiences, which they have developed over time. They are reluctant to have to start from scratch. Luckily, blended and online learning will often utilise material used to support conventional face-to-face teaching, with little or no alteration. This form of learning delivery benefits a great deal from the personal touch that most trainers bring to their face-to-face classes.

Lessons Learnt

From examining various ways of implementing blended or Online Learning at various universities and in various organisations, I know that this change will affect working practices, recruitment, and financial management. The lessons learned so far point to the need to address the following difficulties:

1. Getting policy makers (CEO's and senior management of Corporations) to first of all recognise that they will need an investment in time and effort, if

this change is to be effective. Without their committed support many of the other affected individuals are unlikely to take this change seriously. They need to formulate policy in relation to the priorities given to implementing the necessary change. Above all they should be seen to be enthusiastic about the change and be seen to promote this form of learning delivery. This support must be forcibly transmitted to the ranks of middle management. Too often middle management has distorted or 'watered down' the agreed policy. Where this has happened, or the Policy Makers' support has been seen as half hearted, failure has followed.

2. Many people expect that such a radical change can happen very quickly. One of the major disadvantages is that effective online learning will take time to implement properly. Training Staff need to be trained and to develop online facilitative skills and policies need to be written and implemented in relation to online administration, course accreditation, online behaviour, specialist recruitment, I.T. software needs and many other minor areas. When examining online schemes that have failed, trying to rush the implementation looms high in reasons for failure. Successful implementation of blended or online training involves some change in culture and that cannot be rushed.

3. Participants need to be briefed and if possible be given 'taster' sessions; otherwise they may feel that they are being given an inferior form of learning. Over 90% of my online participants found Blended Collaborative Learning a more rewarding

experience than any form of traditional face-to-face delivery. Successful online schemes undertook serious marketing to their participant groups.

4. Unless briefed and staffed properly, I.T staff may try and block the introduction of any new conferencing system. New systems usually require that the I.T. department need to learn how to manage, support and advise on the system being introduced. Unless a senior member of the I.T department has a good understanding of the needs of the trainers and course participants, they will try and impose a system that they already support or know well. It has been my experience that I.T. staff will give many reasons why existing software will suffice and this is invariably because they see the need from their perspective and not from a instructing and learning point if view. Where they have had their way, it has often led to an unsuitable system being adopted. Remember the introduction of online learning is likely to result in a greatly increased workload for the institution's I.T. department. To cope with this additional work, extra staff, training and resources must be planned, in relation to the I.T. department.

5. Too often supervisors of participants are not considered. Efforts need to be made to make them aware of the benefits of a blended /online earning approach to the organisation. This form of learning often results in the participants being absent from the workplace for less time than if they were on traditional Face-to-face courses, or for short periods of time each day so that thy can still be available for the majority of the working day. Supervisors can be

positively influenced about blended or e-learning, by way of various presentations.

My research leads me to believe that all of the above take time, effort and considerable thought. I believe that it is very necessary if an organisation is to successfully implement this form of learning approach.

Conclusions.

Having worked with staff at a number of universities, higher education colleges and other organisations, I have seen too many trainers who have been expected to develop online skills alone. There is little understanding in many organisations of the knowledge needed to become a successful online course deliverer. To often, trainers are being asked to discover the lessons learned by online pioneering. This results in them making similar mistakes to those of the early pioneers of this medium. Effective online trainer training should make trainers feel confident in delivering successful online training, where completion rates are very high. It should equip them to know when online training is appropriate, and equally important, when it is not likely to be effective. It should give participants practice in giving online feedback and being able to deal with particular problems associated with blended/ online learning, such as information over-load and non-participation, just to name two possible problems that may occur.

The important role of the online trainer in establishing successful online delivery needs to be recognised and provision made for effective trainer training. Society is changing. Younger participants are more at ease with computer conferencing and thus more willing to accept this form of training. Effective online course deliverers are already in short supply and they will be needed if effective learning is to be delivered online.

Having read this section, it will help you to write down at least three things that you found useful and that you might use when training:

1.

2.

3.

Appendix A

Sample Evaluation Sheet (Company Name)

Course Title: _____Location:_____ Date:_/_/_

Name (not obligatory) _____

Please Circle the answer nearest your feelings	Strongly Disagree	Disagree	Agree	Strongly Agree
1. Pre Course				
Promotional material Accurate	1	2	3	4
Course Registration Easy	1	2	3	4
The Course venue information accurate	1	2	3	4
2. Learning Environment	**1**	**2**	**3**	4
I was made to feel welcome	1	2	3	4
The Trainer was approachable	1	2	3	4
There were no distractions	1	2	3	4
The Location was neat and tidy	1	2	3	4
I felt happy to ask questions	1	2	3	4
The refreshments provided were acceptable	1	2	3	4

3. Content

The course materials supported the learning and were up to date	1	2	3	4
The course material was useful	1	2	3	4

4. Presentation

The trainer gave effective presentations	1	2	3	4
The trainer knew the subjects	1	2	3	4
The Learning Objectives were clearly explained & taught	1	2	3	4
The trainer gave effective feedback to participants	1	2	3	4
The trainer promoted involvement & discussion	1	2	3	4
The trainer answered questions effectively.	1	2	3	4
The quality of training was effective	1	2	3	4

5. Relevance

The course has practical value for my work	1	2	3	4
I would recommend this course	1	2	3	4

Appendix B

Trainer Self Assessment

Date _____

Activity	Satisfied with this	Could be improved	Needs work	Priority 1st, 2nd, 3rd
Introducing myself to individual participants				
Being Welcoming				
Ascertaining what Participants want from the course				
Finding out Individual's learning needs & delivering these				
Developing participants' willingness to share ideas and Information				
Making time to talk to individuals				
Listening to participants views				
Identifying Participants' feelings				
Giving information clearly				
Repeating important items				

255

Confronting unrealistic
expectations early

Using group work to
maximise individual
contributions

Using Pauses when asking
questions

Repeating the question asked

Review Visual Aids

Review Course material

Watch for the 'fidget factor'

Learning Objectives achieved

Encouraging feedback from
the participants

Review Progress on priorities by: Date _____

Book References

Mehrabian, A., Silent Messages, Wadsworth, Belmont,California (1971)

Birdwhistell, R. L., The language of the body: the natural environment of words' in A. Silverstein, (ed.), Human Communication: theoretical Explorations (203-220), Lawrence, Hillsdale, NJ (1974)

Gessner, R. (ed.). The Democratic man: Selected writings of Edward C Lindeman. P.166. Boston: Beacon, 1956

Igguden, C., Dunsten, Penguin Random House UK (2017) P.67 ISBN 978-0-718-18144-4

David Meier, The Accelerated Learning Handbook, P16-17, The McGraw-Hill Companies, Inc. 2000

David Meier, The Accelerated Learning Handbook, P48, The McGraw-Hill Companies, Inc. 2000

Peter Honey and Alan Mumford. The Learning Styles Helper's Guide, 2009 TalentLens, a division of Pearson Education Ltd, London, UK. ISBN 9781902899282

Mel Berger and Paul Watts(1994)Management development in Europe, in Managing learning, London, Edited by Christopher Mabey and Paul Iles, P.248, Routledge,

Barry Tomalin and Mick Nicks, 2007, The World's Business Cultures and how to Unlock them., Thorogood Publishing London ISBN:1854183699

John Mole., 2003,. Mind your Manners, Managing Business Cultures in The New Global Europe. Nicholas Brearley Publishing, London ISBN: 1-85788-314-4

Considering Blended Learning References

[1] Robin Mason, (1998) Globalising Education Trends and Applications (p.41) Kogan Page, London ISBN 0-7494-2129-0

[2] Oye, D., Salleh, M. & Iahad, N. (2012) International Arab Journal of e-Technology Vol.2 No.4, June 2012 P. 205

[3] Sloman, M. (2002) Breaking through the e-learning barriers. Training and Development Journal. 56(10) 37-41

[4] Sloman, M. (2002) Breaking through the e-learning barriers. Training and Development Journal. 56(10) 37-41

[5] Ettinger, A., Holton, V., & Blass, E. (2006a). E-learner experiences: key questions to ask when considering implementing e-learning. *Industrial and Commercial Training,* 38(3), 143-147.

[6] Grundry, John (1992) *Understanding Collaborative learning in Networked Organisations*, published in Collaborative Learning Through Computer Conferencing The Najaden Papers Edited by Anthony R. Kaye. Published by Springer-Verlag Berlin

[7] Milner, H and Draffen, I (2000) Learning Support ---The UFI Proposals – A consultative document (p.3) Published by University for Industry, Sheffield

[8] Mallinen, S (2001) *Teaching effectiveness and online learning, in Teaching and Learning Online, pedagogies for New Technologies*, Kogan Page, London

[9] Mason, R (1998) *Globalising Education Trends and Applications*, Kogan Page, London

[10] Eisenstadt, M and Vincent, T (1998) *The Knowledge Web,* Kogan Page, London

[11] Prendergast, G (1997) *Facing up to Radical Changes in Universities and Colleges*, Kogan Page, London

[12] Pincas, A (1996) *The Learning Benefits of Well-designed Computer Conferencing*, Institute of education, London University

[13] Fay, N *et al* (2000) Group discussion as interactive dialogue or as serial monologue: The influence of group size *Psychological Science*, **11**(6), pp 481-486

Index

Workshops Run by the Author

The Author runs half day, one and two day workshops on the followings subjects

1. Using Group Work Effectively
2. Improving how you ask and answer Questions
3. Getting the most from Debriefing learning Activities
4. Effective Presentation and Delivery
5. Body Language
6. Listening Skills
7. Dealing with Difficult Course Participants
8. Implementing Blended or e-Learning in Your Organisation
9. Training the e-Learning/Blended Trainer to be effective

Should any of these workshops be of interest then you can contact the author at:

gplearning@me.com

9 781786 232731